T0265792

The Gift of Rejection fosters inner growth, as rejection impacts us all, regardless of our position in life. Nona teaches us to identify the pain points from rejection and transform them into a beautiful gift that will propel us toward a powerful future.

SARAH JAKES ROBERTS, *New York Times* bestselling author; founder, Woman Evolve

Rejection has devastating long-term consequences in our lives. Nona's transparency and vulnerability in *The Gift of Rejection* will help you find freedom and healing in your own life.

CHRISTINE CAINE, founder, A21 and Propel Women

Rejection can hit hard, breaking your heart when you can't wrap your head around it. But in *The Gift of Rejection,* Nona Jones opens up a powerful new way to see things that turns that pain into a strong foundation for your future. This is a must-read.

ANTHONY O'NEAL, CEO; speaker; author

The message of *The Gift of Rejection* is so needed! Many of us feel shame and pain from the rejection we have experienced. Nona's vulnerability and transparency is a much-needed supplement to help heal the pain and find victory and triumph. You need this book!

CRYSTAL RENEE HAYSLETT, actor; producer; host

Nona has given us a perspective on rejection that we didn't even know we needed. By giving us the gift of her vulnerability, Nona walks us through the pain she's experienced to show us the freedom she encompasses. *The Gift of Rejection* is the guide we need to be freed!

TIM ROSS, podcaster

The Gift of Rejection is a necessary read because no matter how famous you are, how wealthy you are, how beautiful you are, or how powerful you are, rejection still hurts. We all have to face that pain, learn from it, and grow from it to experience the fullness of what it means to be successful. This book is the key to facing the truth that sets you free from the sting of rejection.

NAOMI RAINE, Grammy Award–winning Christian/Gospel artist

I've known rejection. I've felt forsaken. I've been broken. How could any of this be a gift? Seriously! Well, Nona Jones provides a mega paradigm shift that converts pain into purpose, regret into resilience, and hurt into healing. Her message is counterintuitive but true—and it works. Don't miss out on her life-changing message.

LES PARROTT, PhD, *New York Times* bestselling author of *Saving Your Marriage Before It Starts*

Nona Jones has written a masterpiece. *The Gift of Rejection* is an amazing book that shows you how to transform the worst things that happen in life into the best things through the power of perspective. This book is a must-read for anyone seeking to turn their setbacks into stepping stones toward a more fulfilling life.

DEVON FRANKLIN, *New York Times* bestselling author

Nona speaks to the deep pain of rejection that all of us have felt, but she turns that pain into fertile soil for greater blessing. Her book reminds us that sometimes the biggest stumbling blocks can become stepping stones to something beyond what we could have imagined. If you have ever been rejected, spurned, or hurt, this book can open your eyes to how those things can put you on a path to freedom.

DEB LIU, author, *Take Back Your Power*

Many people believe that success makes you immune to the pain of rejection, but take it from me, if you live for people's acceptance, you'll die from their rejection. *The Gift of Rejection* is the key to healing the pain.

LECRAE MOORE, Grammy Award–winning artist

THE GIFT OF
REJECTION

THE GIFT OF
REJECTION

HARNESS YOUR PAIN TO PROPEL YOUR PURPOSE

NONA JONES

ZONDERVAN
BOOKS

ZONDERVAN BOOKS

The Gift of Rejection
Copyright © 2024 by Nona Jones

Published in Grand Rapids, Michigan, by Zondervan. Zondervan is a registered trademark of The Zondervan Corporation, L.L.C., a wholly owned subsidiary of HarperCollins Christian Publishing, Inc.

Requests for information should be addressed to customercare@harpercollins.com.

Zondervan titles may be purchased in bulk for educational, business, fundraising, or sales promotional use. For information, please email SpecialMarkets@Zondervan.com.

ISBN 978-0-310-36829-8 (audio)

Library of Congress Cataloging-in-Publication Data

Names: Jones, Nona, author.
Title: The gift of rejection : harness your pain to propel your purpose / Nona Jones.
Description: Grand Rapids, Michigan : Zondervan, [2024]
Identifiers: LCCN 2024011370 (print) | LCCN 2024011371 (ebook) | ISBN 9780310368274 (hardcover) | ISBN 9780310368281 (ebook)
Subjects: LCSH: Rejection (Psychology)—Religious aspects—Christianity. | Christian life. | BISAC: RELIGION / Christian Living / Inspirational | RELIGION / Christian Living / Calling & Vocation
Classification: LCC BV4509.5 .J655 2024 (print) | LCC BV4509.5 (ebook) | DDC 248.8/6—dc23/eng/20240531
LC record available at https://lccn.loc.gov/2024011370
LC ebook record available at https://lccn.loc.gov/2024011371

Any internet addresses (websites, blogs, etc.) and telephone numbers in this book are offered as a resource. They are not intended in any way to be or imply an endorsement by Zondervan, nor does Zondervan vouch for the content of these sites and numbers for the life of this book.

The information in this book has been carefully researched by the author and is intended to be a source of information only. Readers are urged to consult with their professional advisors to address specific medical or other issues. The author and the publisher assume no responsibility for any injuries suffered or damages incurred during or as a result of the use or application of the information contained herein.

Names and identifying characteristics of some individuals have been changed to preserve their privacy.

The author is represented by Tom Dean, Literary Agent with A Drop of Ink LLC, www.adropof-ink.pub.

Cover and image design: Amanda McIntire, MAC Creative Agency
Interior design: Kait Lamphere

Printed in the United States of America

24 25 26 27 28 LBC 6 5 4 3 2

CONTENTS

PART 1

SPECIAL
DELIVERY

INTRODUCTION

When people look at me, they see a confident woman who appears to have it all together. But I have been deeply wounded by rejection. I imagine you have too. If you're anything like me, you picked up this book because you're hoping for answers, looking for something to heal your pain.

Maybe the rejection happened many years ago.

Maybe it happened last week.

Maybe it happened this morning.

Regardless of when it happened, it hurts.

You can't imagine how being overlooked, disinvited, abandoned, or discarded could be a good thing.

Maybe you're thinking, "Nona, my dad has never said a kind word to me or about me. How is that a gift?"

Or "Nona, my husband cheated on me and left to marry his mistress. How is that a gift?"

Or "Nona, I work harder than anyone on my team, but my boss denied my promotion anyway. How is that a gift?"

Or "Nona, the person I thought was a close friend stopped responding to my calls and texts. How is that a gift?"

Or "Nona, my child no longer speaks to me because I don't approve of their poor choices. How is that a gift?"

While the *act* of rejection isn't a gift, what it can *teach you* about yourself and others *is* a gift. No matter how many positive affirmations you know and no matter how many Scriptures you have memorized, rejection hurts. But pain is only its wrapping paper. The gift is on the inside.

I wrote this book for the same reason that many authors write: I needed it. Rejection is the dull blade that has shaped my character through the years, and if I knew then what I know now, I could have saved weeks, months, and years of residual heartbreak.

In this book, I'll take you to major landmarks on my rejection journey, in particular, three experiences that impacted me personally, romantically, and professionally. Their wounds were so deep they left scars on my heart. Because I can think back today on each one with less pain and more perspective, I am sharing them to help you know you are not alone and there is hope for healing.

I have discovered that no matter who walks away from you, overlooks you, or doesn't want you around, you have the power to harness your pain to propel your purpose. My prayer is that you will soon discover that gift.

CHAPTER 1

LEFT IN THE FIELD

Warning: This chapter recounts memories of sexual
abuse. If you feel uncomfortable while reading,
please proceed to the next chapter.

"You should call your mom more," my husband said over breakfast one morning.

"I've told you. It's complicated," I said as I scooped a forkful of eggs into my mouth.

"No parent is perfect," he said. "I know she's made mistakes. I'm just saying you should call her more. You only get one mom."

I was twenty-two years old and just one year into being married. "Tim, when my mom is in my life, things get really, really hard. She's never apologized for what she let happen to me as a child. She even blames me for it."

"She probably just has a lot of guilt, Nona," he said as he slathered grape jelly onto his toast. "Be the bigger person. Make it right."

My husband was raised in a tight-knit family. Although his family, like every family, had its challenges, his father, mother, and four siblings loved each other. When I married him, I was looking forward to being part of a loving family just as much as I was looking forward to being a wife.

Even before we got married, my husband and I spent every weekend with his parents. When my relationship with him got serious, I started attending his father's church. We had dinner with his parents, siblings, and their families after church every Sunday. Because of their closeness, he couldn't understand why I didn't like to talk to or visit my mom. He couldn't comprehend why a child would be estranged from a parent, and when I tried to explain my complicated and painful history with my mom, his kind heart simply couldn't make sense of it.

After we married and settled into our new home, Tim would regularly encourage me to reach out to my mom, hoping we could reconcile. He truly believed my mom felt sorry for what happened but just didn't know how to apologize. Since we lived only an hour and a half away from her, and because my husband was so insistent, I decided to try to work on the relationship again—*for the hundredth time*. My mom had not yet visited our home, so I planned to drive to her neighboring city and bring her back to spend the weekend with us.

I planned a mother-daughter spa visit, lunch at a favorite restaurant, and some shopping. I became more and more excited with every detail. But when I pulled into a parking space outside her condo, I felt a familiar knot in my stomach. On cue, my heart rate quickened and my palms started sweating. As my body slipped back to its nine-year-old self, I had a realization: time does not heal all wounds.

I braced myself as I walked to her doorstep and rang the doorbell.

"Nona!" My mom smiled broadly as she flung open the door. Her overnight bag was on the ground next to her.

"Hi, Mom," I said while remaining outside. "Have everything?"

"Yes, but let me do one last check," she said as she walked back inside.

"Okay," I said. "I'll take your bag to the car and meet you there."

After a few minutes, I watched her walk up with a smile on her face and pep in her step. I felt a flicker of hope in my heart start to fan into a small flame. "Could this be the day?" I wondered. "The turning point in our relationship?"

I silently prayed for God's help as she slid into the passenger's seat and fastened her seat belt. I prayed that our ninety-minute drive would be a fruitful conversation. I prayed that we would mend the cracks in our relationship. I prayed that I would finally have a mom. I had a lot of resentment and bitterness in my heart toward her, so I planned to talk it through in a respectful way in hopes of arriving at my house with a fresh start between us.

Boy, was I naive.

As we reached the outskirts of her city and the upbeat sound of Bob Marley's "Three Little Birds" filled the air, I took a deep breath and said, "You know, Mom, I really want to build a mother-daughter relationship between us."

"What do you mean?" she asked.

"Talk on the phone and laugh. Take trips together. You know? Enjoy each other. Spend time together. Don't you think it's strange that we don't do that?"

"Not really," she said, shrugging and turning to stare out the window.

"Well, I . . . I really want that. But for that to happen, we have to talk about what happened with Lee."

The mood in the car turned icy at the mention of Lee's name. I sensed my mom's anger rising. I had learned as a child how to sense such things because whenever her temper reached its apex, she would hurl curse words and fists in my direction. This is why, to this day, I am a deeply empathic person. I can feel imperceptible shifts in someone's mood, whether in person or over the phone.

"There's nothing to talk about. That's in the past. I'm not dealing with it."

"Mom, we have to. We have to deal with it," I calmly pleaded.

I knew that going forward was impossible if we didn't first go back. And that meant discussing Lee.

Lee became my mother's live-in boyfriend when I was four years old. Mom had been married to my father for thirteen years before getting pregnant with me, but halfway through her pregnancy, he was diagnosed with terminal stomach cancer and given six months to live. He lived until two months shy of my second birthday. After he died, my mom moved us to the other side of the country, where she met Lee.

Something about Lee frightened me from the beginning, so much so that when my mother's sister passed away and she needed to go to the funeral, I begged her to take me with her.

I didn't want her to leave me with him. But she didn't have enough money for my plane ticket. The very first night she was gone, he sexually violated me.

"You better not tell your mom," he said. "She'll get rid of you. She doesn't want you."

Lee broke not only my body but also my heart. He repeatedly abused me for two years until I worked up the courage to tell my mom. She had him arrested.

But after Lee's release from jail, my mom brought him back home, and he started abusing me again. To make a horrible situation worse, my mom started verbally and physically abusing me, telling me over and over, day after day, "I should have never had you! You're worthless. I never wanted you in the first place."

The cycle of abuse and rejection distorted my sense of self so much that I felt like a piece of trash—good for nothing but being discarded.

FIELD OF REJECTION

The Bible tells us in 1 Samuel 9:15–20 that God chose a man named Saul to be the first king of Israel. He wasn't elected by the people or appointed by a council. He wasn't even the son of a king. God handpicked him for the job by telling a prophet named Samuel that he was the one (1 Samuel 9:17). Unfortunately, Saul had deep insecurities that caused him to seek approval from men more than from God, ultimately costing him his kingship (1 Samuel 13:11–13; 1 Samuel 15:24–26), so God instructed Samuel to visit a man named

Jesse. God had chosen one of Jesse's sons to be the next king. After Samuel arrived in Bethlehem, "he consecrated Jesse and his sons and invited them to the sacrifice. When they arrived, Samuel saw Eliab and thought, 'Surely the LORD's anointed stands here before the LORD.' But the LORD said to Samuel, 'Do not consider his appearance or his height, for I have rejected him. The LORD does not look at the things people look at. People look at the outward appearance, but the LORD looks at the heart'" (1 Samuel 16:5–7).

Samuel assumed Eliab was the one because he *looked* chosen. But God reminded him that his ways are not our ways. Something in Eliab's heart disqualified him for the kingship despite how "kingly" he looked.

> Then Jesse called Abinadab and had him pass in front of Samuel. But Samuel said, "The LORD has not chosen this one either." Jesse then had Shammah pass by, but Samuel said, "Nor has the LORD chosen this one." Jesse had seven of his sons pass before Samuel, but Samuel said to him, "The LORD has not chosen these." So he asked Jesse, "Are these all the sons you have?"
>
> "There is still the youngest," Jesse answered. "He is tending the sheep."
>
> Samuel said, "Send for him; we will not sit down until he arrives." (1 Samuel 16:8–11)

Let's rewind for a moment.

Samuel invited *all* of Jesse's sons to the sacrifice. Seven of them got the memo. One of them didn't. The location of the one who didn't get word was well known by his father.

And yet that son wasn't invited to the sacrifice until the prophet insisted on it.

How is it that seven of Jesse's sons were invited, but the youngest was left out in a field by himself to tend the sheep?

In my experience, the most painful form of rejection doesn't happen by accident. It's intentional. A person makes a conscious decision to overlook you, exclude you, use you, or discard you. And just like it did with Jesse's youngest son, rejection leaves you out in a field of pain by yourself.

ALL MY FAULT

Although I wasn't yet a mother when I picked up my mom for her weekend visit, I couldn't understand how someone could bring their child's abuser back home after locking him up. I couldn't imagine knowing someone hurt my child and then giving them access to hurt them again.

"Mom, you knew what Lee did to me," I said. "You were the one who had him arrested for it. When you brought him back, I felt like you chose him over me. Like you didn't care about me. That hurt me deeply and still hurts now because you've never even apologized for it."

"Well, look, you always wanted me to buy you toys and things, and Lee helped me buy them, so you're as much to blame as the blame you try to put on me."

I was dumbfounded. Her rationale for staying with the man who sexually abused me repeatedly was that I wanted "toys and things." In her warped thinking, it was *my fault* that she stayed with him. But Lee was unemployed for 90 percent of their relationship. They regularly fought over him not contributing to the bills, so her explanation was not only irrational but also a lie. He couldn't have bought me "toys and things" if I had wanted him to, which I didn't.

"Besides," she started, "it wouldn't have happened if you would have just kept your legs closed."

Her words landed on me like a boulder, knocking the wind out of me. We were forty-five minutes away from her house, but I choked back tears of rage, shame, sadness, and shock as I turned my car around and drove back to her condo in silence. She grabbed her overnight bag and slammed the door before huffing back up the walkway to her home. As I reversed out of the parking space with tears blurring my vision, I asked God for the grace to never look back.

When I walked into my house without my mom three hours later, my husband saw the distraught look on my face and jumped up from the couch, asking, "What happened?" But I couldn't even allow the words to cross my lips. I just shook my head and went to lie down as the few tears I had left fell from my eyes. He slid in bed behind me and wrapped his arms around my waist as I fell asleep from emotional exhaustion.

At that time, I could have quoted ten verses on how deeply God loves me, but her words still left me feeling worthless. I could have written a dissertation on how painstakingly perfect God made me even before I was formed in the womb, but her words quickly unearthed the belief that I was defective. The pain of rejection is not soothed by what we know in our heads.

My mom's response left me feeling as if I'd been left out in a field by myself like Jesse's youngest son. As I lay in bed with my shattered heart, I thought about how my mom hadn't made much effort to build a relationship with me as a kid, even though I was her only child. I have no memories of laughing with my mom. No memories of special traditions. No memories of her playing games with me.

Although my mom didn't know how to read while I was growing up because she was expelled from school in third grade, she had a bookcase filled with encyclopedias and other books that people had given her over the years. Those books became my company. I would retreat into them like an escape hatch from the pain I felt in our home. They helped me cope with the uncertainty of my day-to-day life.

Every day, I felt the ache of my mother's absence. When I ran track in middle school and played tennis in high school, she wasn't in the stands cheering for me. I had to catch rides with my classmates' families to get to the games, because my mom was either at work or somewhere with Lee.

When I saw mothers hugging their children at school, I wondered why my mom seemed allergic to me and why she chose Lee over me. I wondered why my mom would go days and weeks without speaking to me as a child, then months and years as an adult.

My mother's rejection weighed so heavily on my heart that it dug a cavernous hole—one I filled with "friends" and boyfriends who couldn't have cared less about me. I latched on to the crumbs of any attention they gave me, often settling for no attention whatsoever. I carried full responsibility for making the relationships work.

I believed I was so worthless that if I made even the slightest demand of someone, they would leave me. The few times I did make an ask of someone, their prompt disappearance proved over and over again that I was disposable. I wanted so badly to be *wanted* that I was willing to be *badly* wanted.

Have you ever been there? Have you ever felt "left in the field" so long that you've lowered your expectations of other people? Instead of expecting fidelity, you just *know* your boyfriend will cheat on you like the others did, so you tell him to at least wear protection *when* he does it, not *if*.

Have you been "left in the field" so long that you're afraid of people walking away if you ask for help? Instead of admitting you're overwhelmed, you lose sleep to complete a work project because you don't want to burden your colleagues.

Have you been "left in the field" so long that you see yourself as worthless? Instead of enjoying your children, you look at them and remember being given up for adoption by your birth mother. You think, "Clearly something was wrong with *me*," because you can't imagine giving up *your* children.

As you think about the fields you have been left in, the field of rejection can serve two purposes. It can be the place where you get discarded *and* the place where you get trained in resilience. Even though someone may have made you feel worthless, God loves to use discarded things to prove he has the final say.

THE TRAINING GROUND

In 1 Samuel 16:13, we learn that Jesse's youngest son was a young man named David. You may remember him from one of the most famous Bible stories in the world—the story of David and Goliath.

David, a young Israelite shepherd boy, defeated the giant Philistine warrior, Goliath, against all odds. And although the battle between David and Goliath often gets the headlines, what happened *before* that event gives us a glimpse of the gift of rejection.

We know from 1 Samuel 16:5–11 that David was left in the field while his father and brothers met with Samuel. As we read further in the story, we learn that David was a regular fixture in the field. In 1 Samuel 16:19, King Saul asks Jesse to send David, "who is with the sheep." In 1 Samuel 17, just one chapter after Saul sends for David while he was left in the field (as usual), we find that famous Bible story of David and Goliath.

People normally jump to the scene where David takes his slingshot and a few smooth stones and sends Goliath to his final resting place, but before that, David's father had sent him to take lunch to his brothers. They were in Israel's army on the day Goliath challenged the Israelites to send their best warrior to fight him. When he heard Goliath making fun of Israel, David turned to Saul and said, "'Let no one lose heart on account of this Philistine; your servant will go and fight him.' Saul replied, 'You are not able to go out against this Philistine and fight him; you are only a young man, and he has been a warrior from his youth'" (1 Samuel 17:32–33).

When I read this scene, I always imagine my two boys when they were young and loved wearing their Power Rangers costumes with the built-in muscles. They would run around the house assuming they could take down any threat because they had "muscles" (pronounced MUS-kulz). Just as I used to look at my fearless little boys, Saul probably looked at the young shepherd boy and patted him on the head with an "Aww, that's so sweet, David."

"But David said to Saul, 'Your servant has been keeping his father's sheep. When a lion or a bear came and carried off a sheep from the flock, I went after it, struck it and rescued the sheep from its mouth. When it turned on me, I seized it by its hair, struck it and killed it'" (1 Samuel 17:34–35).

In other words, David was telling Saul, "These muscles are real. They were built from some hard battles."

He continued, "Your servant has killed both the lion and the bear; this uncircumcised Philistine will be like one of them, because he has defied the armies of the living God. The Lord who rescued me from the paw of the lion and the paw of the bear will rescue me from the hand of this Philistine" (1 Samuel 17:36–37).

Did you catch that? David said he was qualified to fight Goliath because of what happened when he was left alone in the field tending sheep. While alone in that place, neither his father nor his brothers protected him. He didn't have reinforcements to support him. The field that was meant to be a place of his discarding became the place for his training.

When you are living your life to please God, even people's rejection of you will serve God's purpose for you.

When you are living your life to please God, even people's rejection of you will serve God's purpose for you.

David had been left out in that field *by himself* day after day, week after week, month after month, and year after year.

But it was those experiences that created the conditions that helped him train to defeat Goliath. When those lions and bears showed up to attack the sheep, David couldn't turn to his father or brothers for help because he was by himself. He had to fight off animals with no one but God at his side.

David justified his ability to defeat Goliath by saying, "The LORD who rescued me from the paw of the lion and the paw of the bear will rescue me from the hand of this Philistine" (1 Samuel 17:37).

You too can take hope in God's protection.

No matter who left you in the field of rejection, God promises never to leave you nor forsake you (Hebrews 13:5). No matter how long you have been left in that field, Jesus promises to be with you, even to the end of the age (Matthew 28:20).

David's isolation strengthened his confidence to challenge Goliath—not because *David* was big enough but because he came to know that *God* was bigger than Goliath. Whether a parent or a husband or a friend left you out in the field, remember who never left you!

God uses what should have killed us to make us stronger. Not only that, he uses it to help us know without a shadow of a doubt that he is real. He will redeem the pain of your rejection.

As you begin this journey with me, my prayer is that each chapter will equip you to discover the ways rejection has shaped you so you can learn how to receive the gift it wants to teach you. To help you on your way, each chapter concludes with a four-piece toolbox:

RECALL lists the key teaching points from the chapter.
RECEIVE offers a guiding Scripture to contemplate.
RECITE provides a prayer you can pray based on the chapter theme.

REFLECT offers a set of questions to prompt introspection and personal learning.

I invite you to use this toolbox to pause and reflect. Then join me in the next chapter to explore how our past experiences reverberate through the present-day beliefs that shape us.

RECALL

- Time does not heal all wounds.
- The most painful form of rejection is intentional.
- The pain of rejection is not soothed by what we know in our heads.
- We sometimes want so badly to be *wanted* that we're willing to be *badly* wanted.
- A field can be the place where we get discarded *and* the place where we get trained.
- When you are living your life to please God, even people's rejection of you will serve God's purpose for you.
- God will redeem the pain of your rejection.

RECEIVE

The LORD who rescued me from the paw of the lion and the paw of the bear will rescue me from the hand of this Philistine. (1 Samuel 17:37)

RECITE

Lord, this situation doesn't feel good to me, but I trust that you can make it good for me. Give me the patience to endure as you redeem this pain and mold it into a purpose that restores my joy. You are sovereign, and your love for me is absolute. You are more powerful than the greatest adversary I could face. Thank you for loving me.

REFLECT

Take a moment to think about and answer the following questions:

1. In what ways have you felt left out in a field?
2. How did you compensate for feeling alone? What did you do to cope with the pain?
3. How has rejection been an unlikely training ground for building your character or skills?

CHAPTER 2

REJECTED INTO PURPOSE

"We're going to approve a leadership succession plan at the next board meeting, and I was wondering what you would think about being named my successor."

I was three months into serving in a senior executive role for a large nonprofit when the CEO, Sean, asked me this question. I had served on the organization's board of trustees for three years before joining the team full time. My role was designed to build and lead the team responsible for growing the organization's national footprint. It felt like a dream job.

In a nutshell, I was responsible for funding the mission, expanding the mission, and telling people about the mission. Since I loved what I got to do every day, Sean's offer to name me as his successor was easy to say yes to. So I did.

When I first joined the staff of the organization, my peers on the leadership team—Grace (a pseudonym), the chief financial officer, and Larry (also a pseudonym), the chief human resources officer—welcomed me with open arms. They introduced me to their staff and regularly invited me to lunch or dinner, where we enjoyed a lot of laughs over good food. I basked in the glow of their support and friendship and could not have imagined being anywhere else.

That warmth changed when Sean announced his succession plan during our next executive team meeting. After he shared the news, I sensed a negative shift in the room's energy.

"When did you decide this?" Grace asked Sean with a look of confusion.

"Well, the board meeting is next week, and I need to announce it then," Sean said.

"Isn't this something we should have discussed?" Larry asked with a look of angst on his face.

"What is there to discuss?" Sean asked.

"I think something that big should be decided by all of us together," Grace said.

"Not all decisions can be made as a group," Sean said before moving on to the next agenda item.

Although the meeting was tense, by the end of it, we were all laughing again, so I assumed everything was fine.

But I was wrong.

Our national expansion strategy required raising a substantial amount of money from new funding sources, but my team didn't have the expertise we needed and it was too small to support the plan. I put together a PowerPoint presentation that outlined my staffing needs and projected return on investment, then set a time to meet with my peers to secure their support. When I met with Grace to help find some money in the budget, however, I was met with obstruction.

"We don't have any money for new hires right now, especially not fundraising hires. Heck, that's why you're here. To raise the money," she said with a straight face.

I responded by saying I was caught in a catch-22. I needed more people to grow the donor base, but without a bigger donor base, I couldn't build the team. Still, she persisted.

"Like I said, we don't have the money. As the next CEO, I'm sure you can figure it out. And I would suggest you talk to Sean about it," she said with a smirk before turning back to her computer.

I went to Larry next.

"This is too many people," he said after counting the number of employees on my chart.

"Based on what?" I asked. "This is what I will need to support growing into a national organization with a diverse funding base."

"I mean, it's bigger than my team *and* bigger than Grace's team. I can't support this."

"I didn't design it with your teams in mind. I spoke with peers at other major nonprofits who have done what we're trying to do, and this is what it will take. Besides, it will happen in stages. I just need a few new roles in the short-term to build the foundation."

Larry gave the diagram one more glance before sliding it back across the table and saying, "In my professional opinion, I think you need to start small. It's too big."

I left his meeting dumbfounded and then went to Sean, hoping he would help me.

After listening to my rationale for the team investment, he said, "Listen, Larry and Grace already walked me through the budget restrictions, and we won't be able to fund this anytime soon."

I felt my heart rate climb as I realized they had used my

conversations with them to undermine my request for more staff. I tempered the rising emotion in my voice and said, "Well, in the absence of the team I need, I need to get really clear on your expectations of my performance."

"I would say to just do what you can with what you have. We will fund your team as you find resources to support more staff."

I went back to my office in an emotional fog. I felt like a target had been placed on my back. I got the impression that both Grace and Larry wanted to be named as Sean's successor.

Nevertheless, I decided to put my head down and get to work. I had to find a way to do my job in the absence of the team I needed. Grace and Larry had seemed like such great partners and advocates for me in the early days, but after Sean told them he intended to name me as his successor, they left me out in the field. I felt alone, unsupported, and rejected.

Although I felt defeated in the moment, time has helped me understand that God used that rejection as part of his plan for my life.

FROM PALMS TO NAILS

Matthew 21 shares the powerful account of Jesus's entry into Jerusalem the week before his crucifixion. It's often described as "triumphal" because the people give him a victor's welcome and receive him with excitement:

> The crowds that went ahead of him and those that followed shouted,
> "Hosanna to the Son of David!"

"Blessed is he who comes in the name of the Lord!"

"Hosanna in the highest heaven!"

When Jesus entered Jerusalem, the whole city was stirred and asked, "Who is this?"

The crowds answered, "This is Jesus, the prophet from Nazareth in Galilee." (Matthew 21:9–11)

The people following Jesus were so jubilant that the entire city began to wonder who everyone was so excited about. People adored Jesus, celebrated Jesus, and honored Jesus—until they didn't. Not long after, Jesus was taken prisoner and brought before Pontius Pilate: "At that time they had a well-known prisoner whose name was Jesus Barabbas. So when the crowd had gathered, Pilate asked them, 'Which one do you want me to release to you: Jesus Barabbas, or Jesus who is called the Messiah?'" (Matthew 27:16–17).

Mark 15:7 describes Barabbas as a murderer who was justly imprisoned and sentenced to death. Pilate offered the crowd two options, but the "chief priests and the elders persuaded the crowd to ask for Barabbas and to have Jesus executed" (Matthew 27:20).

The Jewish leaders successfully turned the hearts of the crowd against Jesus Christ. The same people had laid palm branches at his feet only a few days earlier. When Pilate asked them what he should do with Jesus, the same mouths that had sung, "Hosanna in the highest heaven!" responded with, "Crucify him!"

How is it possible that someone who had a triumphal entry into the gates of Jerusalem would find himself hanging from a wooden cross just outside the gates five days later?

How is it possible that many of the same hands that laid palm branches at Jesus's feet would be the same hands raised to vote "aye" in nailing him to the cross?

How is it possible that the very people who accepted Jesus as their Lord and Savior could be the same people to reject him as a criminal?

People's acceptance is fickle. One day, they think you're the best thing since sliced bread. The next day, they want to cut you like sliced bread. Things get especially complicated when someone is offended by others' acceptance of you.

Jesus was rejected by a group of priests and elders who felt slighted by his popularity with the masses. Matthew 21:23 says, "Jesus entered the temple courts, and, while he was teaching, the chief priests and the elders of the people came to him. 'By what authority are you doing these things?' they asked. 'And who gave you this authority?'"

In other words, they wanted to say, "Who do you think you are, Jesus?" They had worked for years to earn their place of prominence among the religious elite, but Jesus had the audacity to come onto the scene out of a "nowhere" town called Nazareth (John 1:46), and people accepted him as the Messiah. In turn, the chief priests and elders rejected Jesus because people's acceptance of him was too much for their fragile egos to bear.

Have you ever experienced this? Maybe your family moved to a new town when you were young and you had to start at a new school where you didn't know anyone. As you befriended people, some kids started picking on you and calling you names for no reason. They rejected you out of jealousy simply because others accepted you.

Or maybe you started dating a new guy, but after you posted fun pictures with him, your best friend stopped taking your calls. She rejected you out of jealousy simply because he accepted you.

Or maybe you were selected for a new management training program at your job. As you moved up in leadership, your colleagues stopped inviting you out for happy hour. They rejected you out of jealousy simply because leaders accepted you.

Jesus was fully God *and* fully human, so I suspect he felt as much pain from rejection as we do. I can imagine he wrestled with the same questions we ask ourselves: Why are they treating me like this? What did I ever do to them? Why me?

Before he was taken captive, Jesus went before God and asked, "My Father, if it is possible, may this cup be taken from me. Yet not as I will, but as you will" (Matthew 26:39).

The humanity of Jesus felt it all—the isolation, the betrayal, the anxiety.

Still, Jesus knew his rejection was part of **In God's hands,** the purpose of his birth. He understood that the **rejection is** gift of rejection can build purpose out of pain. In **redirection.** God's hands, rejection is redirection.

FALL FROM GRACE

Without the funding I needed to staff my fundraising team, I knew I had to get creative. I spent the next year researching and applying for corporate grants that funded the work of organizations supporting vulnerable families. As money came in, I pieced together my new development team bit by bit.

Our organization was virtually unknown to major corporations and foundations at the time. I knew that to accelerate progress, I had to build our national brand recognition. But how? And how to do it for *free*? We didn't have money for fancy marketing campaigns.

I saw an advertisement from a local marketing agency announcing a contest to support a rebranding project for a nonprofit. I applied and was elated when we won. I worked closely with their team to develop a fresh, new brand image for our organization. When I rolled out the new website and marketing materials across the organization, everyone loved them. Especially Sean.

"This is the exact right thing we need, Nona! You pulled a rabbit out of the hat on this one, for sure!"

A few weeks later, I received an email announcing the Obama administration's new advisory group for vulnerable families.

I reached out to a couple of lobbyist friends and asked if they had any White House connections. Within two weeks, I was in touch with a senior advisor serving the advisory group. I flew to Washington, DC, for a meeting and shared about our organization's work with vulnerable families in our state. I also shared about our ambition for national expansion. To my great delight, they agreed to connect me with the right people on the Hill.

Over the coming months, I visited the White House every other week, meeting with high-level officials in key departments serving children and families. I was invited to testify before the Senate Judiciary Committee, and as part of that opportunity, I brought one of the families that had graduated from our program to share their story. Two weeks later, I received a phone call from an advisor to the Senate Judiciary Committee Chairman informing me that, thanks to our compelling testimony, they would be funding a new grant for family support programs like ours. I was over-the-moon excited.

After the grant was posted, I hired a consultant to work with me and our team to write the strongest application possible. One month later, Sean called me late at night and asked if I was sitting or standing.

"Standing right now. Is everything okay?"

"Nona, I just received an email saying we've been awarded $800,000 from the grant you applied for! This is huge! This is historic! I'm just so proud. So, so proud," he shouted into the phone.

When I hung up, I dropped to my knees and thanked God. I had spent a grueling year of positioning our organization in the best light possible with key officials in Washington. We had gone from being virtually unknown in DC to being funded by the federal government in what can only be described as sound barrier–breaking speed. It was quite literally a miracle. Not only that, but I had secured several six-figure multiyear grants from major corporations along the way too.

When Sean emailed news about the federal grant to the staff and the board of trustees, my inbox overflowed with congratulatory messages. But two people's names were conspicuously absent: Grace and Larry.

Whenever I shared in executive team meetings about my

progress in DC, I would catch a glimpse of Grace rolling her eyes or Larry smirking. The tension was palpable.

"Nona, I need to tell you something," a colleague said over lunch one day. "You have some haters working against you."

"Haters? What do you mean?"

"Well, I was in a meeting about you coming to speak to the team, and Larry said you probably wouldn't have time because you're only interested in jetting off to the White House. The way it was said made me uncomfortable. You've never been anything but humble and gracious. It rubbed me the wrong way."

"Wait. What!"

"Yeah, I know. It was clear to me that he's jealous of you."

"Jealous . . . of me? For doing my *job*?"

"No, not jealous of you for doing your job. Jealous of you for doing your job *well*. And that's not all. Apparently, Grace has been working to convince Sean not to fund your budget request for next year."

"Why in the world would she do that?"

"Nona, you're outshining them. They've been planting seeds with people in the organization. Saying you're building your own empire instead of the organization's."

At the time, I wasn't sure what to do with my colleague's caution, but when performance reviews came around two months later, Sean's demeanor had changed.

"Nona, we need to have a talk," he said.

"Sure. I'm excited about all the momentum I've built over the past—"

"Well, that's the problem, actually," he said. "*You* have built a lot of momentum, but I don't see how your team has been empowered to build momentum."

I was dumbfounded. "What team, Sean? Every request I've made for resources has been met with a no, whether from you or Grace or Larry."

"We're resource constrained."

"No, *I'm* resource constrained. Grace has a fully staffed team and so does Larry, and they *still* got more head count approved in the budget. Not only did I get the federal grant, but we also have multiple large corporate grants too, and our donor development infrastructure is being upgraded as we speak. Our brand is new and fresh, *and* my inroads into new states are bearing fruit. All of this without the team I said I needed from the beginning."

Sean sat in silence for a moment, then said words I will never forget.

"You know, Nona, when I look at all you've done, I think you're a good individual contributor, but you're not a leader."

As I sat across from him, I felt tears well in the corners of my eyes, but I forced myself to hold them back. Just a couple of years earlier, he had thought so highly of me that he named me his successor. I had exceeded expectations in every way possible, but Grace and Larry had systematically turned Sean's heart against me out of jealousy.

When I gathered my things and walked out of Sean's office, I felt a release in my spirit. An invisible weight that had been holding me down suddenly detached itself. As I prayed about it the next morning, I heard the Lord say, "This assignment is over."

"Over? How, Lord? I'm just getting started."

"It's over."

My mind raced with the inconceivable idea of leaving

the job I loved. "If it's over, what do you want me to do next?" I asked.

"Resign at the end of the fiscal year."

It was mid-April. The fiscal year ended June 30, only two months later. How in the world could I possibly leave a job so soon with no plan B? I had far more questions than answers, but I knew the voice of God.

"He said to resign June thirtieth," I told my husband in a shaky voice.

"Are the bills resigning too?" he asked with eyebrows raised in shock.

"I don't know. But I *do* know this is what God said."

My husband looked down at his hands for a few minutes, then said, "Well, God will make a way. If this is what he said, he will make a way."

My husband and I both understood: even when we can't see the "why" of a rejection, God uses it to position us for purpose.

THE FINAL SAY

Right before jealous religious leaders had Jesus taken captive in the garden of Gethsemane, Jesus said, "My soul is overwhelmed with sorrow to the point of death" (Matthew 26:38). The weight of rejection crushed his soul.

Have you ever been there?

Maybe your fiancé left you for someone else, and the weight of his rejection has broken your heart.

Maybe your father doesn't speak to you because your

mother was pregnant with you during their divorce. The weight of his rejection has broken your spirit.

Maybe your coworkers make fun of you because of your speech impediment. The weight of their rejection has made you feel ostracized.

When Jesus's captors showed up in Matthew 26:47, they were led by one of his closest friends. A disciple he loved. A disciple he had eaten with. A disciple he had traveled with. Matthew 26:49–50 says, "Going at once to Jesus, Judas said, 'Greetings, Rabbi!' and kissed him. Jesus replied, 'Do what you came for, friend.'"

Judas not only pointed out Jesus to the captors but also kissed him—a sign of friendship, affection, honor, and loyalty. Jesus responded in an unusual way and called him *hetairos*, which is Greek for "comrade." Although I can't imagine calling someone who betrayed me by that name, Jesus did. He labeled him a friend and fellow soldier, someone who shared the same mission and objective.

The next day, Jesus endured a torturous beating ahead of his crucifixion, and as his mangled, bloody, and broken body struggled to carry the cross to Mount Calvary, people lined the streets to spit on him, slap him, and throw trash at him. But just when the religious leaders thought they had won, God proved that their rejection was simply a tool for his ultimate mission. John 19:28–30 (NKJV) says, "After this, Jesus, knowing that all things were now accomplished, that the Scripture might be fulfilled, said, 'I thirst!' Now a vessel full of sour wine was sitting there; and they filled a sponge with sour wine, put it on hyssop, and put it to His mouth. So when Jesus had received the sour wine, He said,

'It is finished!' And bowing His head, He gave up His spirit."

Jesus spent thirty-three years on earth, with only three of those years in public ministry. But while everything seemed to be falling apart in his earthly life, everything was actually falling into place as the eternal strategy of God unfolded. With three words, God turned rejection on its head. "It is finished" cast a signal to every principality, power, and ruler of darkness in the spiritual realm:

From this moment forward, you are defeated!
From this moment forward, the only ground you will
    have will be the ground you are given!
From this moment forward, anyone who believes in
    the name of Jesus Christ will have the victory, and
    no matter what scheme the enemy may devise,
    it will fail!

Just when the religious leaders thought they had won, God's divine plot twist showed they were nothing more than supporting characters in the play he had written.

God had the final say then, and God has the final say now. Rejection is under subjection to Christ.

DIVINE DETOURS

When June 30 arrived, I asked Sean to meet with me at the end of the day. I had rewritten my resignation letter at least a hundred times, whittled from five pages down to three sentences. I slid it across his desk and said, "I have enjoyed my time here and am grateful for the faith you have placed in me. I have decided to pursue other opportunities and will be resigning effective two weeks from today."

The color drained from Sean's face. "Resigning? In two weeks? Why?"

"It's just time for me to pursue other opportunities."

"Where are you going? Can I do anything to convince you to stay?"

The answer to the first question was that I had no idea, but I simply said, "I appreciate that, but no. I'll share my next move soon."

"This is a shock, Nona. Wow. Well, can you give me more than two weeks?"

"If you feel more time is needed after reviewing my plan, I will honor it so you feel comfortable."

When I left our meeting, I felt light and heavy at the same time. I felt light because I knew I was doing what God had told me to do. But I felt heavy because God hadn't told me what he was planning for me on the other side of my obedience. To my surprise, it took only twenty-five minutes for his will to be revealed.

As I drove home, my cell phone rang, displaying an unfamiliar 650 area code and the words *San Francisco, California*. Although I assumed it was a telemarketer, the Holy Spirit compelled me to take the call.

"Hello," I said into the phone.

"Yes, is this Nona Jones?" a friendly woman asked.

"It is. With whom am I speaking?"

"This is Kara. I'm calling from Facebook."

"Facebook? Facebook doesn't call people. Who is this?"

"No, really. I'm calling from Facebook. I work on the recruiting team, and your name was given to me as someone I need to talk to. I don't know if you've been following the news, but Mark just changed our company mission to focus on community building. One of the communities we want to invest in serving is the global faith community, and we were told you were someone who could help us."

"Oh? That's interesting. Well, I'm driving right now, but can you send me some information? I'll take a look when I get home."

"Of course. I'll email it to you now. Just give me your best address."

I assumed they were putting together an advisory group or committee, but when I opened my email later that evening, there was a link to a job description for the newly created role of global head of faith partnerships. My jaw dropped.

Twenty-five minutes after I resigned from the job I loved because the pain of rejection left me seeking God's will for my next move, God caused the world's largest social media company to offer me a job out of thin air. Although I later learned that it typically took four months for a candidate to go through the selection process for a role at the company, two weeks after that initial phone call, without ever stepping foot on campus, I received an offer letter for more compensation than I asked for. Two weeks after *that*, I started the job that would forever shift the trajectory of my life.

After I joined the company, I learned that a friend of mine who was an executive at the time had recommended me for the job, but he told recruiting, "Nona loves her current job, and I don't think we can get her to leave, but I can't think of anyone better to do this, so let's at least try." He had that conversation with recruiting the same month God told me to resign from my job, but my friend never said a word to me.

I had many job offers come my way during my time with the nonprofit, but because I loved what I was doing, I turned them down without a thought. That changed when my colleagues turned against me. Although God didn't cause or endorse their rejection of me, he used it to redirect me.

True to his word, God knew the plans he had for me, even when I couldn't see them.

RECALL

- God can use our rejection as part of his plan for our life.
- People's acceptance is fickle.
- In God's hands, rejection is redirection.
- God uses rejection to position us for purpose.
- The weight of rejection is soul crushing.
- Rejection is under subjection to Christ.

RECEIVE

"For I know the plans I have for you," declares the LORD, "plans to prosper you and not to harm you, plans to give you hope and a future." (Jeremiah 29:11)

RECITE

Lord, show me how you have used my rejection as a divine detour so I can see your goodness at work in my life. Help me to remember that, just as you orchestrated the rejection of Jesus for the divine purpose of my freedom, you can orchestrate my own rejection for the purpose you created me for.

REFLECT

Take a moment to think about and answer the following questions:

1. How has rejection caught you off guard?
2. What surprised you about it, and what did it teach you about yourself and others?
3. How has rejection been a divine detour for you?

DANGERS UNSEEN

"I'm nominating you for this program, Nona," Ms. Levy said while handing me a piece of paper in her office. "I think you would represent the school well."

Ms. Levy was my eleventh-grade guidance counselor. She had nominated me for a citywide leadership program that would bring together top students for a six-month intensive with high-profile leaders in the city. The program's goal was to cultivate the next generation of business leaders, civic leaders, and elected officials. Students were selected because of their strong academic record and extracurricular leadership. I was elated to be chosen.

On our first program day at City Hall, we students were scheduled to meet with city council members, the mayor, and the sheriff. When I walked into the meeting room, I immediately noticed one of the students. He was tall and athletic with smooth chocolate skin. Every time he smiled, he flashed a set of braces as two dimples dotted his cheeks. A half dozen students surrounded him, beaming in his direction. I wasn't sure who he was or what he was saying, but the other students were enraptured by him. They laughed at whatever jokes he was telling them and nodded vigorously at whatever points he was making.

I found a seat near the front and made small talk with the kids around me before the program director kicked off the day with a welcome.

"You were each nominated to represent your school because you represent the future of leadership for our city," said Mrs. Donaldson, the program director. "This program will help you discover and unleash your potential for greatness."

When she asked for volunteers for a mock city council meeting, I raised my hand, and she selected me to represent the fictional District 3.

"The utility company wants to increase rates for the fifth year in a row, and you have to decide whether to approve it or not."

As I reviewed my district brief, I noticed that a sizable percentage of my constituents apparently struggled to pay their bills. After the conversation went back and forth, I proposed an idea: "Instead of increasing rates across the board, can we ask the utility company to come up with different rates based on how much electricity a person uses? If people found ways to use less electricity, that would reduce the utility company's costs and also encourage people to use less so they pay less, right?"

The other three mock council members and the mock mayor nodded in agreement. Mrs. Donaldson responded, "Great idea, Nona! Way to think creatively."

At the break, I walked over to the beverage table and poured a cup of lemonade, then I heard a voice say, "Hi, Nona!" I turned to see dimples-braces-chocolate guy smiling at me.

"Oh, hi . . ." I couldn't remember his name.

"Barry. It's Barry," he said with a smile.

"Barry, yes! I'm so sorry." I started to walk away, but he continued.

"Really impressive role-play there. That was a great idea."

"Thank you. My district had a lot of poor people, so I wanted to find a compromise," I said.

"Yeah, that was smart," he said. "A lot of politicians just look out for their own interests. My dad was a state senator for many years. I plan to run for office one day."

"That's really cool," I said. "I never considered running for office before today, but I just might."

"You should," he said. "You're smart. And pretty. You would win easily."

I felt my cheeks get warm and thanked God that my brown skin hid evidence of what I was feeling.

"Thank you. That's very nice of you to say," I said.

"Not nice. True," he said. "I'll see you around."

At the end of the day, Barry asked me for my phone number. We talked on the phone a few times a week between sessions, and by the time the program graduation arrived six months later, we were officially together. His father got him a summer internship with a state legislator five hours away in South Florida, but we talked almost every day while he was gone. Considering his charm, brilliance, and the vision of greatness he had for himself, I felt like the luckiest girl on earth.

When he came back to town to visit during his summer away, he asked to take me out to the movies. I was so excited that I bought a special outfit and counted down the days. But an hour before he was supposed to pick me up, he called to tell me that a family emergency had come up. I was bummed, of course, but I made the best of the situation by inviting a few of my friends to go to the movies instead.

As we stood in line waiting to buy tickets, I glanced over at the next line. My heart stopped. Barry was standing in line holding hands with another girl. After he bought their tickets, he looked back and saw me. His mouth dropped open, and he looked mortified. When one of my friends saw him too, she grabbed me by the arm and said, "I'm so sorry, Nona! He's a jerk!"

I don't know that I would have felt any different had Freddy Krueger ripped my beating heart out of my chest like in *A Nightmare on Elm Street*. Barry had been stringing me along. He rejected me for someone else. I felt betrayed, used, and discarded. When Barry called me repeatedly over the following week, begging to apologize face-to-face, I deleted every voicemail without calling him back.

In the crucible of the moment, I thought I would never recover from the pain. My head spun as I replayed the lie of our relationship. I couldn't have imagined anything good coming out of something so painful, but I would eventually learn a lesson that would stay with me for years: the gift of rejection comes wrapped in packaging we least expect.

THE NEED FOR CONNECTION

As a concept, the gift of rejection seems nonsensical. Gifts are *good*. They make us happy. We anticipate them with joy. Rejection is none of that. It's painful. It makes us sad. We brace ourselves for even the *possibility* of rejection.

Sociologists and biologists have long pointed to the importance of social connection for human survival and the strong correlations between community and longevity.[1] Connecting with others brings biological, psychological, emotional, and spiritual benefits. When we believe we are accepted by someone, we feel safe enough to trust them. That's why rejection hurts so deeply.

It crushes the belief that we were wanted.

It damages the faith that we were chosen.

It doesn't just injure our pride, it also breaks our heart.

It doesn't just bruise our ego, it also shatters our hope.

In an interview with *Scientific American*, scientist Matthew Lieberman writes,

> Languages around the world use pain language to express social pain ("she broke my heart", "he hurt my feelings"), but this could have all just been a metaphor. As it turns out it is more than a metaphor—social pain is real pain. . . . We tend to assume that people's behavior is narrowly self-interested, focused on getting more material benefits for themselves and avoiding physical threats and the exertion of effort. But because of how social pain and pleasure are wired into our operating system, these are motivational

ends in and of themselves. We don't focus on being connected solely in order to extract money and other resources from people—being connected needs no ulterior motive.[2]

Research shows that when social acceptance is withheld, people report actual physical pain. And when we dig into the cause of that pain, we find it has a name: rejection.

TYPES OF REJECTION

Rejection happens in a variety of ways and relational contexts.

FAMILY REJECTION: This occurs when family members withhold the basic human needs of attention, affection, and love. Family members include parents, siblings, aunts, uncles, cousins, or grandparents, and their actions can take the form of abuse, neglect, abandonment, ostracization, and more. Since this rejection involves the people most engaged in the formative years of our lives, it can have the most devastating effect on our sense of self-worth.

PROFESSIONAL REJECTION: This occurs when people we work for or with prevent us from advancing professionally. Someone withholds opportunities for us to develop our skills or build our networks with clients, colleagues, or leaders at our company. Since this rejection affects our livelihoods, it can lead us to question our competence.

SOCIAL REJECTION: This occurs when people in our social sphere ostracize, alienate, humiliate, or bully us. It can happen at school, at work, or in any other community setting, including civic and social clubs. Since this type of rejection affects our relational networks, it can be particularly isolating and hurtful. People who challenge the status quo of a particular group often experience social rejection. For example, questioning friends about their political views or offering dissenting opinions can lead to social rejection. The pressure to avoid social rejection sometimes causes people to conform to social expectations, even when they don't agree.

ROMANTIC REJECTION: This occurs when our love interest in another person is either unreciprocated or is explicitly denied. We express affection for someone, but they immediately rebuff us, or after we've invested time into a relationship, our partner ends it against our wishes. This type of rejection is especially painful because it can leave us feeling betrayed and blindsided.

THE UNMASKING

When we anticipate even the *possibility* of not being accepted by others, we try to shield ourselves by wearing masks. We use them to hide the parts of our true selves that we believe put us at risk of rejection.

Maybe your mask is "perfect wife." You were raised to believe that a *real* wife always has a delicious home-cooked meal on the table for her husband at the end of the day. Never mind that you hate cooking. You worry that your husband (and his mom) will look down on you for not living up to the role you were given. To compensate, you search for recipes and make meals you can post on social media with the caption, "Nothing but the best for my man!" You were never taught how to cook and have no interest in it, but isn't that what a perfect wife does?

Maybe your mask is "perfect friend." You can barely pay your bills, but you worry that your friends will walk away if you don't buy them things. Whenever one of them has a birthday, you charge an expensive gift to your almost maxed-out credit card. You would much rather save and pay off your debt. But isn't spending money what a perfect friend does?

Maybe your mask is "perfect Christian." You secretly struggle with alcohol addiction, but you worry that if you tell people at church, they might ostracize you. Whenever the church doors open, you're there. But your public persona is inconsistent with your private battle. You need help and long to share your pain, but the potential cost of being shunned keeps you quiet.

Imagine being part of a church community where people celebrated vulnerability and supported you through your struggles instead of condemning you.

Imagine having friends who bought *you* gifts on your birthday and celebrated every bill you paid off by taking *you* out for dinner.

Imagine being married to a man who knew you didn't like to cook, so he was the first to prepare a meal or order takeout.

When you're understood and valued, you feel *seen* for who you are, *known* for what you need, and *still* loved because of it. You feel safe. You feel empowered to disarm your defenses. You feel enabled to drop your mask.

When you're understood and valued, you feel *seen* for who you are, *known* for what you need, and *still* loved because of it.

But what do you do when the person who disarms and unmasks you isn't who you think they are?

46

DANGERS UNSEEN

Deep rejection happens when you let your guard down and take off your mask and then a person walks away from you. The real you is on display, which means they are walking away from who you *really are*. You wonder what you should have done differently or what mask you should have worn to be accepted. But what if their rejection is protecting you from unseen danger?

Maybe your father never wanted anything to do with you as a child. You internalized his choice as evidence that something was wrong with you, but after he passed away, you found out he had molested several female family members when they were children.

Maybe you were turned down for a shiny new promotion you had been vying for in a separate division at work. You internalized the decision as evidence of your being a failure, but months later, everyone in that unit got laid off, including the person selected for the job you wanted.

Maybe a group of popular kids made fun of you in high school. You internalized their cutting remarks as evidence of your unworthiness, but at your fifteen-year reunion, you found out most of them struggle with drug and alcohol addictions that carried over from binge partying in high school and college.

In the heat of the moment, all you felt was pain. But when the full truth came to light, you realized that the rejection served an unforeseen purpose. You look back on the situation and think, "I'm so glad that happened."

Just like a man named Joseph.

FEASTING IN THE FAMINE

About six hundred years before David was born, a young man named Joseph was born.

He was the beloved son of a man named Jacob, whose name God changed to Israel in Genesis 35:10. Joseph is introduced to us in Genesis 37:3, which says, "Now Israel loved Joseph more than any of his other sons, because he had been born to him in his old age; and he made an ornate robe for him." In other words, Joseph was Jacob's favorite. He made this obvious to his other sons: "When [Joseph's] brothers saw that their father loved him more than any of them, they hated him and could not speak a kind word to him" (Genesis 37:4).

What did Joseph do in a situation where his siblings hated him because his father was quite open about his favoritism? Well, he acted with humility toward his siblings, of course. Wrong! Enter the first plot twist.

Joseph had a dream in which his brothers were bowing down and worshiping him. A person with common sense might tuck the dream in the back of their mind. But apparently Joseph said to himself, "I bet my brothers would *love* to hear about it!" After he told them, things took a rapid turn for the worse, and his brothers sold him into slavery in Egypt.

After some heartbreaking events—Joseph was wrongly accused of rape and forgotten in prison while innocent of all charges—God orchestrated his liberation. Pharaoh had a dream none of his advisors could understand. But a member of his royal court knew Joseph had a gift for interpreting dreams, so he recommended him to Pharoah. Joseph correctly interpreted the dream, and so Pharaoh made him second-in-command over Egypt (Genesis 41:39–40).

Thirteen years after his brothers sold him into slavery, Joseph was appointed prime minister of the land they sold him into. And not only that. Pharoah's dream foretold seven years of abundance, followed by seven years of famine, so Joseph worked diligently to prepare the country. During the years of plenty, he stored huge quantities of grain, so when the famine started, the Egyptians had an abundance of food and enough left over to sell to others (Genesis 41:57).

At the height of the famine, Joseph's brothers showed up begging for food. As they bowed before him and pleaded for help, they didn't recognize him. But he definitely recognized them.

They were hungry. Emaciated. Desperate.

Had it not been for their rejection those many years before, he would have been one of them. Instead, he was full. Strong. Living in abundance.

Joseph's life flashed before his eyes. All the resentment, bitterness, confusion, and anger melted away as he began to see the mighty hand of God at work in his life. All the pain, heartache, and tears started to make sense. He eventually revealed his identity to his brothers, and in the end, he said, "You intended to harm me, but God intended it for good to accomplish what is now being done, the saving of many lives" (Genesis 50:20).

Even when rejection doesn't make sense, God can make it count for our good.

NEVER SAW IT COMING

When Facebook hired me to lead its global faith partnerships team, I immediately hit the road. I crisscrossed the United States to meet with pastors, imams, rabbis, and priests. It was a wonderful immersion into the different ways people practice faith. I became good friends with one pastor in particular who became something of a father figure to me. He was also a mentor to many young pastors around the country.

One day he texted and asked if I could give him a call about an urgent issue. I had no idea that my entire life was about to be flipped upside down.

"Hi, Bishop! How can I help?" I asked him.

"Thanks for calling, Nona," he said in an unusually strained voice. "This is a really sensitive matter, and I hope you can help. One of the young pastors I've been mentoring for a few years needs to have his Facebook page taken down."

I furrowed my eyebrows in confusion. I had countless people ask for help getting their Facebook page back *up* after it had been taken down by our systems, but I'd never had someone ask to have it taken *down*.

"I don't understand, Bishop. Why would he want that?"

"Well, it isn't that he wants it. It's that people are posting derogatory, mean comments on his page. He's dead."

"Oh no, Bishop. I'm so sorry. And I'm surprised people would do that on a dead person's page. Can you email me the link and I'll see what we can do? I can't make any promises. We don't take down pages unless they violate our community standards, but I'll escalate it and have the team take a look."

"I understand. I just appreciate you for being willing to try to help. It's a bad situation. Really bad. He made some horrible decisions, but I don't want him to be remembered for the worst things he ever did," he said.

"I'll see what's possible. Send me the link, and I'll get it to the right people."

After we hung up, he texted me a link to the dead pastor's profile. When I clicked it, Barry's face was staring back at me. It was the same face that stared back at me when I caught him at the movies with another girl in high school.

"This can't be right," I said to myself. As I scrolled through the comments, I fell into a twilight zone of shock.

Comment #1: "Cheaters deserve whatever comes to them. Good riddance!"

Comment #2: "See, this is why I don't go to church! How did he call himself a pastor, out here living a double life!"

Comment #3: "I hope his wife makes it. This is all so sad and unnecessary. He was so selfish."

The comments numbered in the thousands. The story had apparently gained national attention, but because I didn't watch anything except *Food Network*, I had been oblivious to it. I searched his name on Google and found countless news articles. As I read the details, I found it hard to breathe.

Barry had been shot by a woman he was having an affair with. According to reports, she showed up at Barry's home, and his wife let her in because she knew her. As the woman started to leave, she turned around and yelled at Barry,

"You broke my heart!" then pulled out a gun and started shooting at the couple. Both Barry and his wife were taken to the hospital, but only his wife survived.

After his death, multiple women reported having affairs with Barry. They said he told them he was getting a divorce because his wife was crazy. The news articles showed pictures of his wife, and as I stared into one, I saw the face of the young woman who was standing next to Barry in line at the movies. I felt my head get hot. I thought he had cheated on me with *her*, but maybe he was cheating on *her* with *me*. Just as she didn't see me that night, she might have had no idea about the other women he had been cheating on her with over the years.

I imagine Joseph felt a similar mixture of emotions when he stared into the faces of his brothers that fateful day. He realized that all the pain, heartache, and hurt he had experienced over his thirteen-year journey from rejected brother to falsely accused slave to powerful politician was used by God to redirect him to safety and provision. Although Barry's former wife has made a full physical recovery since the shooting, I can only imagine the psychological and emotional trauma she is still wading through years later.

I can't help but think about how close I came to being on either side of that situation.

What would have happened if I had answered his calls and accepted his apology? Could I have ended up being her, or one of the many women Barry strung along?

Every article I read left me feeling a profound sense of thankfulness. The more I learned about Barry's double life, the more gratefulness I felt toward God. My gratitude drowned the bitterness I had been carrying toward Barry and helped me understand Joseph's reaction to seeing his brothers that day. What Barry meant for evil God meant for good. In God's hands, rejection is often protection.

Instead of seeing rejection only as something to lament, what if it is something to embrace too?

In God's hands, rejection is often protection.

OPEN THE EYES OF MY HEART, LORD

"That could have been me, Lord."

In the week after I learned about Barry's murder, I couldn't stop thinking that it could have been my name in the news. I found myself praying and speaking with God often to help process my emotions.

My friends and I could have gone to any movie theater that day. We even passed by several others on our way to that one. We could have gone at a different time. I could have been so focused on my friends that I didn't see him with that other girl.

The coulda, shoulda, wouldas of the situation shook me to my core.

"You allowed me to be there at that exact moment to see what I saw. Thank you, Father."

In my spirit, I began to hear the loving words of God: "Nona, you have been looking at rejection all wrong, and because of this, you have been carrying a root of bitterness in your heart. You brace yourself in expectation that people will reject you, even when they don't."

I remembered the time when I had been out with friends and suggested we eat at a particular restaurant, fully expecting them to shoot down my idea. When they agreed to it, I was confused because I expected them to reject it.

Or the time when I applied to a statewide program for business leaders called Leadership Florida, fully expecting my application to be denied. When I got accepted, I was floored because I expected them to reject it.

Or the time in college when I told a friend that I thought a guy was cute, and she turned around and told him. I felt embarrassed, but the bigger shock came when he said I was cute too and asked me out. I had expected rejection over and over. The surprise was being accepted.

"I know. But I don't know what to do. I try to forgive people for hurting me, but the pain persists."

"Do you still feel bitter toward Barry?"

"Not at all. I'm so grateful that I don't think I could ever feel bitter toward him again."

"Right, but you only feel that way because you have the proof that I protected you. Up until now, you have harbored bitterness because you took his rejection personally."

I had to admit to myself that God was right. I thought I had forgiven Barry before learning of his murder, but I had still been bitter. A year before his murder, he messaged me on Facebook, and I simply deleted the message without responding. It was the right thing to do as a married woman, but seeing his face in my inbox also just made me angry. I was still bitter and wanted my silence to hurt him the way he had hurt me those many years ago.

"How do I forgive *for real*, Lord?"

"It starts with faith."

"But I have faith. I placed my faith in you many years ago."

"Did you? What is faith?"

"Hebrews 11:1 says, 'Faith is confidence in what we hope for and assurance about what we do not see.' It's being so confident in who you are that we believe without proof."

When the word *proof* left my lips, the weight of truth settled on me. I had felt grateful toward God not because I trusted him to work the rejection for my good *in the absence* of proof but because I had *evidence* of his goodness toward me. I had the *receipts*. As the realization overtook me, I felt deep humility.

Have you ever experienced this?

Maybe the mother you idolized called you "stupid" because you didn't get accepted to college for the nursing degree she wanted you to have. After she shut you out of her life, her isolation forced you to go out on your own. In the absence of her expectations, you leaned into your love for painting. Now when you look back at your life, you realize that building your art gallery is worth significantly more than the nurse's salary she wanted you to have.

Maybe the tattoo of your former pimp's name on your shoulder reminds you of a time when running from the pain of childhood abuse left you on the streets, selling your body. Since becoming a Christian, you have openly shared your testimony with others who feel that their past disqualifies their future. When you look back at your life, you realize that hundreds of women and men in your community have found hope by hearing about your story of rejection.

"Wow, Lord. I'm so sorry." I prayed. "I was bitter toward

Barry because I saw his rejection as the final outcome. And to make matters worse, my bitterness wasn't just at him. If I'm honest, I was angry at you too. I blamed you for letting it happen. I didn't feel grateful until I saw the proof that his rejection protected me from a future I couldn't see."

"Nona, I promised to work all things together for your good. I didn't promise that it would *feel* good. I promised that it would *be* good. In my hands, rejection is a gift."

"I can see how Barry's rejection was a gift. I can even see how my mother's rejection ultimately made me the resilient person I am today. But how do I deal with the pain of rejection when it happens? How can I see rejection as a gift when the pain is fresh?"

"The answer is simple—and hard. It requires living by faith and being committed to seeing rejection as a gift. Although a gift is freely given, the receiver has to be open to it. And here's the key: rejection is a gift that will make you *better* if you open it or *bitter* if you don't."

At that time, I had *never* thought of rejection as a gift. Ever. But when I paused to reflect on the lessons it had taught me about myself and others, I had to admit that the overwhelming evidence pointed to it as a gift. Instead of taking rejection personally, I could take it purposefully.

Part of me was eager to let God teach me how to embrace rejection as a gift, but another part of me was worried about the price it would cost. One thing I know about God is that he always develops our character through pressure.

I'm sure you've experienced it.

You pray to God for peace, and next thing you know, you find yourself reading an eviction notice.

You pray to God for joy, and next thing you know, you find yourself battling depression after your best friend deserts you.

You pray to God for hope, and next thing you know, you find yourself staring down a terminal diagnosis.

The book of James encourages us to "consider it pure joy, my brothers and sisters, whenever you face trials of many kinds, because you know that the testing of your faith produces perseverance" (James 1:2–3). In other words, we are encouraged to rejoice in our trials because our character grows as a result.

I knew that submitting myself to God's training through rejection essentially guaranteed more rejection would come. But I also wanted to get free from the pain of past *and* future rejection.

I no longer wanted to be subject to the pain of people overlooking me.

I no longer wanted to be subject to the pain of people not inviting me.

I no longer wanted to be subject to the pain of people walking away from me.

Still, I yielded to God, knowing I was in store for even more pain. I had the blessed assurance that he would work it together for my good and his glory.

RECALL

- The gift of rejection comes wrapped in packaging we least expect.
- Rejection doesn't just injure our pride. It breaks our heart.
- Even when rejection doesn't make sense, God can make it count for our good.
- In God's hands, rejection is often protection.
- Instead of taking rejection personally, take rejection purposefully.
- Rejection is a gift that will make you *better* if you open it or *bitter* if you don't.

RECEIVE

The Spirit of the Sovereign LORD is on me,
　　because the LORD has anointed me
　　to proclaim good news to the poor.
He has sent me to bind up the brokenhearted,
　　to proclaim freedom for the captives
　　and release from darkness for the prisoners,
to proclaim the year of the LORD's favor
　　and the day of vengeance of our God,
to comfort all who mourn,
　　and provide for those who grieve in Zion—
to bestow on them a crown of beauty
　　instead of ashes,
the oil of joy

instead of mourning,

and a garment of praise

instead of a spirit of despair.

They will be called oaks of righteousness,

a planting of the LORD

for the display of his splendor. (Isaiah 61:1–3)

RECITE

Lord, right now the pain of my rejection feels all-consuming. I can't imagine how you could make beauty out of the ashes of my pain, so I ask you for the grace to trust you and to believe you can do what feels impossible. Restore my sense of worthiness, despite what feels like evidence to the contrary.

REFLECT

Take a moment to think about and answer the following questions:

1. What type of rejection has hurt you the most—family, professional, social, romantic, or other?
2. What role has forgiveness played in your journey to heal from rejection?
3. How has God protected you in your rejection experience?

PART 2

INSPECTING THE GIFT

INTRODUCTION

Before we can move forward in healing from the pain of rejection, we must first go back and understand its nature. In *The Art of War*, Chinese military general and philosopher Sun Tzu shares a powerful strategy for warfare: "If you know the enemy and know yourself, you need not fear the result of a hundred battles. If you know yourself but not the enemy, for every victory gained you will also suffer a defeat. If you know neither the enemy nor yourself, you will succumb in every battle."[1]

Although I believe rejection can become a powerful ally in our personal growth, it can seem like an enemy at first. General Tzu suggests that if you don't understand yourself *or* your enemy, you will always lose. If you understand only *yourself*, but not your enemy, you will lose as often as you win. But when you understand your enemy *and* understand yourself, your victory is assured. His military strategy doesn't map perfectly onto human experience, of course. But it still offers valuable insights. This next part of the book is designed to help you understand what rejection is, how it happens, why it happens, and how the pain of it gets expressed through your thoughts, feelings, and actions. Although I'm not a therapist, we're going to take a few steps into the thorny rose bushes of rejection in hopes of equipping you to go deeper with a professional, if needed.

The more you understand rejection, the better positioned you will be to defeat it. This is my goal for you.

If you are in the United States, visit www.PsychologyToday.com to find a therapist. If you live outside the United States, visit www.InternationalTherapistDirectory.com. Let's explore together.

THE ROOT OF REJECTION

I believe we are all born with an internal GPS that leads us to look to our parents for love, approval, and safety. Attachment theory suggests that for normal emotional and social development to occur, young children need to have a healthy relationship with at least one primary caregiver. While a relationship with our father is deeply important, a mother plays a critical role in our early years. Researchers have conducted studies on how the degree of safety and predictability mothers create early in their child's life affects the child's later life.

In *Being There: Why Prioritizing Motherhood in the First Three Years Matters*, psychoanalyst and parenting expert Erica Komisar shares research on how critical a mother is to the first three years of a child's life. "The more you're with your baby," she writes, "the more you're present, physically and emotionally for your baby, the less stressed that baby is and the less stressed the mother is."[1] Biologically, this makes sense. Most of the time, mothers are the ones who birth, nurture, and nourish us.

According to attachment theory, there are four predominant styles of connection: secure, avoidant, resistant, and disorganized. For the purposes of this chapter, I will focus on two: secure and avoidant.

According to researchers, if a mother demonstrates the *secure* attachment style by responding to her baby's distress with patience, care, and sympathy, that baby tends to mature into a child who feels safe and exhibits positive social interactions with others. The attached child is able to count on their mother for consistent love, approval, and safety. But when babies experience rejection from their primary caregivers, particularly mothers, the impact is disastrous for their sense of safety and self-worth later in life.

When a mother demonstrates the *avoidant* style by responding to her baby's distress with hostility, agitation, and irritation, the baby tends to demonstrate higher levels of social avoidance as they grow into childhood. They will even learn to self-soothe to minimize their displays of negative emotion. As they grow older, they demonstrate avoidant behaviors with others too. They are often labeled as "emotionally unavailable" or "emotionally detached."

Can you relate? Maybe you live behind an invisible wall that prevents people from getting too close to you. Although people *think* they know you, they know only what you allow them to see. You avoid conversations that seek to uncover your fears, hopes, or desires. Your defense mechanism is rooted in being ridiculed for "weakness" as a child.

Or maybe you withdraw when you feel yourself getting emotional. When you feel angry, depressed, or anxious, you avoid connection with others. You tell yourself that sharing would be a burden to them, but your assumption is rooted in childhood rejection.

Or maybe you are hypercompetitive and overaccomplished. You throw your energy into achieving and treat it as the anesthetic for a pain you can't define. You know that getting attention requires doing something worthy of people's admiration because, as a child, you rarely got it unless you achieved an award.

According to Dr. Diane Benoit, a professor of psychiatry at the University of Toronto, "Beginning at approximately six months of age, infants come to anticipate specific caregivers' responses to their distress and shape their own behaviours accordingly (eg, developing strategies for dealing with distress when in the presence of that caregiver) based on daily interactions with their specific caregivers."[2]

Research has repeatedly shown that the way a primary caregiver does or doesn't love, approve of, and protect their baby is highly correlated with how the child learns to respond to *others* as they grow up. It shapes their personality in powerful ways. Babies experience the absence of love, approval, and protection as rejection.

In *Adult Children of Emotionally Immature Parents*, Dr. Lindsay C. Gibson offers case study after case study of adult children raised by distant, self-involved, or demeaning parents. In all cases, the result was the same: people who experienced parental rejection early in life continued to struggle with the impact of their rejection later in life. Even in cases where the adult child ended up married to a supportive spouse or attained professional success, they still struggled with the echoes of rejection.

Dr. Gibson shares the story of a woman named Charlotte:

Charlotte . . . finally accepted a friend's repeated invitations to enter a short story into a writing contest. She was sure the judges would reject her work, even though she was a successful newspaper journalist. To her astonishment, she won.

For Charlotte, this stirred up painful memories of all the times in childhood when she was criticized and shamed by her parents for trying to stand out. Her parents weren't capable of emotional support and instead found reasons to disparage her accomplishments. Now, even as she was thrilled about her award, she simultaneously felt terrified that someone would step forward to mock her or expose her as undeserving.[3]

The rejection we experience as children distorts the way we see ourselves into adulthood. Even if we had an idyllic relationship with our parents, being rejected by educators, classmates, neighbors, or friends also molds our early identity. As we experience multiple rejections in the same area of our identity—how we look, how we talk, how we perform in school—we start to believe we're defective.

Were you often the last kid selected for a team at recess? Were you never selected at all? You may have come to believe something is wrong with you. Notice how, as an adult, you hold your breath when teams are spontaneously being formed at work during a team-building exercise. The residue of rejection from the playground has left a smudge on your heart, so when you get picked last for work teams, you see it as further evidence that something is wrong with you.

Were you part of a blended family, and your half-siblings reminded you often that you weren't biologically connected?

You came to believe you didn't belong anywhere. Notice how, as an adult, you describe yourself as a loner and avoid joining social groups. The residue of rejection by your family has left a smudge on your heart, so when people don't invite you to be part of their group, you see it as evidence that you don't belong anywhere.

Were you a student whose teachers said your poor grades and bad behavior meant you would never amount to anything? You eventually came to believe you were a failure. Notice how, as an adult, you disqualify yourself from opportunities before others have a chance to. The residue of rejection by your teachers has left a smudge on your heart, so when you get fired from job after job, you see it as evidence that you're a failure.

When you get overlooked, disregarded, or discarded as an adult, you don't search long to answer the question *why*. You simply look inside your heart and answer: "I was rejected because I am defective."

THE REJECTION TALK TRACK

Our inability to release ourselves from the emotional, mental, and psychological pain of rejection is caused by the "talk track" we keep looping in our mind. A talk track is a set of statements that automatically play after something triggers them. We often don't even realize they are playing.

Imagine taking a tour of a local history museum. The docent hands you a set of headphones and encourages you to press the red button at each installation to learn more as you walk through. When you arrive at the first exhibit, you press the red button and—voilà—you hear a beautifully narrated description of the exhibit. When the recording ends, you press the button again and hear the narration start over. After repeating this process a few times, you hardly need the narration because you have it memorized.

This is what happens when people's words about us get embedded in our hearts and minds. If the same criticism is repeated enough, we memorize it in our psyche, and it becomes our own talk track.

After being called "fat and sloppy" so often by your mom, all you see in the mirror when you try on new clothes at Nordstrom is a fat and sloppy person.

After being called "lazy and worthless" by your wife, all you can hear after a job rejection is the phrase *lazy and worthless*.

After being called "stupid and dorky" by your classmates in middle school, all you can think when you aren't invited to the office party is, "Why would they want a stupid, dorky person like me there, anyway?"

For some of us, it isn't other people's *words* that create our rejection talk track. It is rejection *itself* that fills in the blanks.

After your husband leaves you for a younger woman, the talk track says, "Nobody wants me."

After your pastor appoints someone else to the position you applied for, the talk track says, "I'm not good enough."

After your child runs away from home and gets addicted to drugs, the talk track says, "I failed as a mom."

After years of reflecting on Barry's rejection, I can now see that, while he did cause me harm, it wasn't what he did that hurt me most. It was the talk track I used to explain *why* he hurt me. I told myself I shouldn't have been surprised. After all, it was me who wrongly dared to believe I was worthy of acceptance in the first place, even though my mother told me I wasn't.

"How could I ever think Barry would choose me when he had better options?" I said to myself.

Forget that Barry was a cheater. I accepted responsibility for his choice to cheat on me, because I was defective. I wasn't enough. And where did I get this idea from? From the mother who chose her boyfriend over me. Do you know what it feels like to be rejected by the people who are supposed to accept you unconditionally?

Maybe you were the product of a one-night stand. Your mother eventually got married, but her husband regularly reminded you that you should be grateful he took in *someone like you*. Although your mother hears what he says to you, she never intervenes. You begin to believe that something *is* wrong with you. You *are* defective.

Or maybe you have a speech impediment or lack of coordination. The others in your family are scholars and athletes, but you required remedial classes and couldn't run fast without tripping over yourself. You remember the disappointment in your father's eyes when he asked how *someone like you* ended up in the family. You began to believe that something *is* wrong with you. You *are* defective.

Or maybe you got pregnant in high school and wore your shame like a coat. Your parents ostracized you and called you "fast," and your aunts and uncles refused to let your cousins anywhere near you for fear that your "looseness" was contagious. As you look into your baby's eyes, all you see staring back at you is proof that something *is* wrong with you. You *are* defective.

Rejection makes us view ourselves through the disapproval of others. We come to expect rejection. Though we're still hurt when it happens, we explain it away as something we knew was going to happen because we're defective.

Even rejection's deepest, darkest pain can become a beautiful testimony of God's grace toward us.

But even rejection's deepest, darkest pain can become a beautiful testimony of God's grace toward us.

BEFORE THE OIL

I want to take us back to the young shepherd boy we met a few chapters earlier. The Bible says little about David's life before he was anointed king of Israel, but there are lessons we can learn from what it *does* say.

Though David's father, Jesse, takes center stage in 1 Samuel 16, he is first introduced in Ruth 4:17. There we learn that Jesse was the son of a man named Obed, and Obed was the son of two pretty well-known lovers in the Bible: Ruth and Boaz. Jesse is the grandson of Boaz, a wealthy Bethlehemite man who feared God.

We know a lot about Jesse. But who was David's mother?

Her name is curiously absent from David's story. There isn't even a passing reference to her or her genealogy. And yet her existence is revealed in key ways throughout Psalms.

David is commonly thought to be the author of many psalms, but only about seventy-five of them identify him as such. One of them is Psalm 51, where he writes, "Behold, I was brought forth in iniquity, and in sin did my mother conceive me" (v. 5 ESV). Although Bible scholars debate whether he is referencing only his spiritual condition, I can't help but think he's talking about the circumstances of his actual birth.

Psalm 69 lends more credence to this idea. David writes, "I am a foreigner to my own family, a stranger to my own mother's children" (v. 8). Is it possible that David's mother's name is never mentioned because he was conceived illegitimately? When Samuel asked Jesse to invite his sons to the special sacrifice, did he leave David out in the field tending sheep (1 Samuel 16:11) because David represented something he wanted to forget?

Do you know what this feels like? For others to view you as "damaged goods"?

Maybe your mother was the mistress of a married man. He begged her to abort you, but she kept you in hopes that he would leave his wife for her. Instead, he cut off contact because you represent a secret he wants to keep hidden.

Your best friend from your small town suddenly stopped wanting to hang out with you after she went to college in a big city. You represent a past she wants to get away from, so she moved on to more "sophisticated" friends at her new school.

Your husband rarely asks you to join him for social gatherings with his work colleagues and their spouses. After having three children, you gained a lot of weight, and he regularly reminds you of how beautiful you *used* to be.

I wonder if David was left out in the field by himself because his father and brothers viewed him as damaged goods too.

When the prophet Samuel saw David's brother Eliab, he thought, "Surely the LORD's anointed stands here before the LORD" (1 Samuel 16:6). Samuel was impressed by the man's appearance. But God reminded Samuel that what matters to humans is not what matters to God.

Jesse had accepted and approved of Eliab, but God had not. By contrast, David's father and brothers had shunned, ostracized, overlooked, and discounted David, but when it came time to decide who would be the next king, God looked at qualifications Jesse didn't see.

Though several of David's brothers were in Israel's army on the fateful day when Goliath challenged them to a one-on-one fight, none of them volunteered for the opportunity. Could it be that their father had created such a comfortable life for them that they didn't feel prepared? Although we don't know that for sure, we learn in 1 Samuel 17:34–37 that David's time alone tending those sheep trained him in ways that his brothers had never been trained.

David's courage was born under the pressure of having to fight off lions and bears by himself. And, because of that, he didn't fear Goliath the way his brothers or the other members of the army did.

People reject us based on outward appearances.

They reject us based on financial status.

They reject us based on educational status.

They reject us based on vocational status.

They reject us based on attributes beyond our control.

But God? He sees our heart. Although you can make an evil heart look good to *people*, you can't make an evil heart look good to *God*.

A STAR IS BORN

I have always loved science—not only biology, physics, and chemistry but also biochemistry, geology, and astronomy. While some people think there is a tension between science and faith, I believe the insights science provides only further confirm the sovereignty of God. When I look up at the night sky, for example, I marvel at the number of bright, twinkling stars dotting the vast blackness and wonder, "How did they get there?"

Scientists believe that stars form through a complex process involving gas, dust, and a molecular cloud that collapses on itself. The force of gravity creates an immense amount of pressure, which causes nuclear fusion. Put another way, stars are born under pressure.

On a much smaller scale, I've experienced this process. My first job was a newly created middle management role at a Fortune 100 company. Frankly, I wasn't qualified for the job. I was hired as the quality assurance analyst for a claims processing department I had never worked in, so how was I supposed to ensure quality for something I had never done? I decided to teach myself in a few weeks what most people take three years to learn.

Stars are born under pressure.

I pored over process manuals and spent countless hours shadowing the people I was supposed to be quality checking. I charted workflows and created process maps. I developed best practice guides and one-pagers to give myself and others quick references. And sure enough, by the end of one month, I was proficient.

My manager was blown away, and her boss was impressed too. I was twenty-two years old when they recommended me for our corporate leadership development program. By the end of it, I found myself in an executive leadership role. People started to refer to me as a "rising star." Although I relished the accolades, I couldn't shake a nagging dissatisfaction. Nothing I did was ever enough. I still felt inadequate.

Do you know what this is like?

Maybe you need a spotless house because you can rest only if everything looks perfect.

Maybe you're pursuing another degree because having more letters behind your name will make you feel like you "belong" in your professional circle.

Maybe you've been on a new trendy diet because being at 8 percent body fat doesn't feel as good as 6 percent.

No matter how much you clean, how many degrees you attain, or how much fat you burn, you never feel content, because a voice in the back of your mind tells you it's not enough and *you're* not enough.

In my case, no matter how much I achieved professionally, I was never satisfied. In the back of my mind, I always heard the whisper, "Nobody wants you, Nona." Every accolade felt hollow. The harder I worked to impress people, the more pressure I felt to perform. I threw myself into my work headfirst, but not because I was excited about the future I was building. I did it because I was trying to silence the voice of rejection from my past.

I achieved success not by running toward my future but by running from my past.

While it is true that stars are *born* under pressure, it is also true that stars can *burn* under pressure. The same pressure that activated my potential was the same pressure that burned me out.

When the root of your rejection is left unattended, the resulting pain and confusion creates pressure that pushes us into relationships and situations that leave us unfulfilled. This is why learning to identify rejection is a necessary step in your healing.

RECALL

- Babies experience the absence of love, approval, and protection as rejection.
- Repeated rejection solidifies the belief that we're defective.
- Rejection makes you view yourself through the disapproval of others.
- Stars are born under pressure.
- Success can be achieved by running toward your future or running from your past.

RECEIVE

See to it that no one falls short of the grace of God and that no bitter root grows up to cause trouble and defile many. (Hebrews 12:15)

RECITE

Lord, show me the root of rejection in my heart. Take me back to the place where the seed was first planted so I can begin to remove it. Help me to cancel the bitterness in my life and replace it with your everlasting grace.

REFLECT

Take a moment to think about and answer the following questions:

1. What is the talk track in your mind? What repeated thoughts attempt to explain why you've been rejected?
2. What criteria do some people use to decide whether to accept you? What criteria does God use?
3. In what ways has rejection caused you to run from your past?

CHAPTER

EXPRESSIONS OF REJECTION

"Hi, Nona. Do you have a few minutes to chat? The nominating committee just met, and I want to get your thoughts on something."

I was sitting in my office when I got this text message from Brandon Moore, the executive director of a statewide association of utility companies. I was serving on their board of directors.

"Sure, Brandon. Can you call in ten?"

Unlike other board members, I was twenty-five and relatively new to the utility industry.

"Thanks for taking my call, Nona," Brandon said. "The nominating committee put together our slate of officers for the next two-year term, and they want to nominate you for vice president."

"Me?" I asked incredulously. "Oh, wow. I haven't been on the board long, Brandon. I'm sure there are others who have been on longer who would be great."

"Of course. We have a great board, but they unanimously agreed that you would make an excellent vice president. If you accept, you would become president-elect, making you next in line to be board president."

After a long pause, I said, "Wow, Brandon. I'm honored. Truly honored."

"Awesome news. I'll let the committee know. Thanks, Nona. I'm looking forward to working even more closely with you."

A few weeks later, after the board officially voted and a press release was distributed, a friend sent me a link to a news article from a prominent statewide newspaper. After reading it, I was surprised to learn that my election at this statewide association made me the first Black person and the youngest person ever to serve as president-elect. Congratulatory emails started pouring in.

"You're a rock star!"

"Keep shining bright!"

"Way to go, superstar!"

At the national conference of state utility organizations that year, I was given the prestigious Robert E. Roundtree Rising Star Award in recognition of my leadership as a young utility executive. The smiles, handshakes, compliments, and hugs were plentiful. But when I returned to my hotel later that evening, the talk track in my mind had replaced every kind word I'd heard that day. Instead of feeling accomplished, I simply felt like a fraud.

That award doesn't change the facts. They probably gave it to you because they ran out of worthy people to recognize. You're just a leftover.

I sat the beautiful glass trophy on my dresser and stared at it while thoughts of unworthiness filled my heart and mind. Loud echoes of childhood rejection drowned out the compliments and congratulations. I had worked hard for these accomplishments, but none of them mattered. On cue, as always, the chorus of accusations replayed in my mind.

Who do you think you're fooling? You're not anything special.

If your own mother didn't care about you, why would a room full of strangers?

Your shiny trophy doesn't mean anything. No one really knows who you are, and no one cares either.

Running from the pain of rejection had led me into the arms of awards and recognitions. But those arms never hugged away the hurt. They simply reinforced the need to do more, because the more I achieved, the more I realized what I hadn't achieved. I was running on a hamster wheel, trying to reach the elusive point of acceptance. I thought the only way to prove I mattered was to achieve bigger and better things. I was successful but unfulfilled. I didn't realize it at the time, but fleeing from the pain of rejection always led me in a circle—back to the empty place I started.

I needed to achieve something that would prove I had value once and for all. I had not yet learned: nothing you can accumulate around you will fill a deficit within you.

> Nothing you can accumulate around you will fill a deficit within you.

WHAT HAPPENED TO YOU?

I once led the marketing team for a statewide network of alternative schools for girls. The students had been suspended and expelled from traditional schools for various reasons, but after enrolling in our program, their lives were radically changed for the better. My team and I would collect their stories and share them broadly to tell of the organization's impact.

I once sat down with a thirteen-year-old girl named Jocelyn to hear her story. She came to our program after being expelled from school for fighting repeatedly. She had a hair-trigger temper and would respond to the slightest sign of disrespect with a ferocity exceeded only by Mike Tyson. But when I sat with her in her counselor's office and asked her to tell me why she was fighting, her answer was illuminating: "I don't want to fight," she said. "I just get so angry. I feel so angry."

"So if you don't want to fight, why do you fight?" I asked.

"It's like something comes over me. I think when people do anything mean to me, it reminds me of my father," she said as tears began to form.

When we hear about kids getting suspended or expelled from school for bad behavior, we can naturally think, "What's wrong with them?" When kids steal, fight, curse, and more, we might believe they should be punished for their behavior. But after spending many years working in juvenile justice, I have learned that things are never as simple as they seem.

"Can you tell me why, Jocelyn? What reminds you of him?"

"My father was a mean man. He was hardly around, but when he was, there was always fighting. If he didn't like something, he made us pay for it."

I noticed a darkness descend over her countenance as she dredged up memories.

"This one time, he . . . he . . . he made me and my younger sister kneel on thumbtacks while he beat us. He used a belt and his fists. I don't even remember what we did."

As Jocelyn recounted one traumatic story after another, I thought about the many times she had been suspended from school for fighting. The many times she had likely been called a "problem" by teachers and administrators. The many times people had defined her by her worst behavior: defiant, aggressive, out of control. But sitting across from me that day was a young girl whose father had rejected her in horrific ways.

A little girl whose father had forced her to stifle her screams of pain.

A little girl whose father had forced her to call herself "stupid" and "whore."

A little girl whose father had made her feel worthless and helpless.

Her father's rejection had molded her into a person she didn't even want to be.

The way we show up in the world is often a by-product of our experiences. The pain of rejection shapes us like clay.

Maybe you are the life of the party. People love having you around because you never let the conversation lull and you make sure everyone has a good time. You learned at a young age that no one wants to hear your problems, so when you crawl into bed from exhaustion every night, you don't share anything with your spouse. Rejection molded your exuberant personality as a defense against isolation.

The pain of rejection shapes us like clay.

Maybe you feel uneasy around people. When someone asks to hang out, you turn them down with the excuse that you already have plans. Although you yearn for connection with others, you're suspicious of their intentions because your parents often left you by yourself as a child. Rejection molded your antisocial personality as a defense against abandonment.

Maybe you are delaying marriage until you "make it" in your career. You're already at a higher level of leadership than most of your classmates, but you can't rest until your name is at the top of the organizational chart. Your teachers said you would never amount to anything, which fueled your ambition to prove them wrong. Rejection molded your hyperambitious personality as a defense against unworthiness.

When the pain of rejection is left unaddressed, as it was in Jocelyn's life, it affects the way we show up in the world. And when the person who rejects us expresses no remorse, the pain can become deeply rooted as bitterness. While anger and bitterness are often thought of as interchangeable emotions, they are quite different.

You can think of anger as an episodic emotion that tends to fade with time. If a driver cuts you off on your way to work, for example, you might feel angry enough to hurl insults at them, but by lunchtime you've forgotten about what happened. Bitterness, on the other hand, is a seething hostility that lingers long after the cause. It seeps into relationships that have little or nothing to do with the initial hurt.

Maybe the person who cut you off drove a Honda Accord, and now every time you see a similar car, you follow it to see if it's the same driver so you can set them straight. That's *bitterness*.

Or maybe your college boyfriend broke up with you when he met a new girl, and six years later, you curse out your husband's secretary so she knows he's off-limits. That's *bitterness*.

Or maybe your aunt spread a hurtful lie that you stole your grandmother's money, and a year later you refuse to answer anyone's calls or attend the family reunion. That's *bitterness*.

The rejections we experience often loop in our minds, periodically reminding us of the hurtful experiences we've had. Bitterness is an instant emotional replay of the events that hurt us.

While anger may lead you to share an upsetting experience with others to get them to *understand*, bitterness leads you to get them *on your side*. If someone dares to see the situation from a different viewpoint, you might feel compelled to end your relationship with them.

This is why God cautions us against bitterness.

Hebrews 12:15 says, "See to it that no one falls short of the grace of God and that no bitter root grows up to cause trouble and defile many." When rejection happens, the grace and power of God *is* present and ready to help us. But first we have to receive it.

When you find out your parents and siblings went on a cruise without you, you can choose to let grace lead your response. Cursing everyone out may feel good in the moment, but if that bitter root causes your kids to avoid their cousins, you will have fallen short of the grace God gave you.

When you find out your child's father has a new girlfriend, you can choose to let grace lead your response. Going to her house and threatening physical harm if she comes near your kids may feel good in the moment, but if that bitter root causes your child's father to stay away from you and your child, you will have fallen short of the grace God gave you.

When you find out your colleague took credit for the project you worked on together, you can choose to let grace lead your response. Bursting into your manager's office and degrading your colleague might feel good in the moment, but if that bitter root causes your manager to view you as a loose cannon, you will have fallen short of the grace God gave you.

With God's help, we can prevent bitterness from taking root. Even when it's hard. Even when it hurts. If we don't, the weight of our bitterness will cause collateral damage.

The pain of rejection makes some of us turn outward and explode. Others turn inward and implode. But whether we explode on others or implode on ourselves, the result is the same: hurt people hurt people. Before we can open the gift of rejection, we have to recognize how rejection is expressing itself in our lives.

EXPLOSION

"I never saw it coming."

Barbara shook her head with tears in her eyes as I sat in her living room after the court hearing. Until then I had gotten to know her only from a distance, as my husband served as a Big Brothers Big Sisters mentor to her fourteen-year-old grandson, Matt.

When Matt was eighteen months old, Barbara stopped by her daughter Sandy's apartment one day to check on him. After she had knocked for a few minutes, the neighbor stepped out of the next apartment.

"Sandy's gone again," she said. "Look, I've been trying to help take care of Matt, but I've got five kids of my own. I can't keep him. My food stamps can't stretch to feed another mouth."

Matt's mother would regularly disappear for days, chasing the next high.

"How long she been gone this time?" Barbara asked.

"I ain't seen or heard from her in two weeks. He's been with me a few days a week since he was born. I can't do it no more. I'ma have to call social services to come get him."

"Oh no! Please don't. Look, I'll take him."

Barbara had four children who were all in some form of trouble. Two of her daughters were addicted to drugs, another was a drug dealer, and her only son was in prison for life for murder. She had been married to Matt's grandfather for thirty-five years before he died of alcoholism. He was a physically, verbally, and sexually abusive man who raped his daughters multiple times.

Sandy ran away from home at twelve years old and had her first baby at thirteen. She had four children before Matt, and they all ended up in foster care from being neglected. By the time she gave birth to Matt, Sandy was addicted to various drugs and didn't know who his father was because she had been selling her body to fund her drug habit.

After Matt's grandmother took him in at eighteen months, his mother would show up at her house every other month and make promises about having him come to live with her. As the years went by and the unmet promises piled up,

Matt realized his mom loved her drugs more than him. In the pain of rejection, he began acting out.

Matt got expelled from middle school for fighting and ended up at a school for emotionally and behaviorally challenged children. Although teachers and counselors told his grandmother he needed intensive therapy, she didn't think his pain was that serious. Deep down inside, she refused to believe that his behavior had anything to do with her daughter, because that would require admitting it had something to do with her *own* negligence. She signed him up for Big Brothers Big Sisters hoping a mentor would help him calm down.

As my husband told me about Matt's behavioral and academic challenges, I knew it would only be a matter of time before his pain caused him to explode in a way he couldn't recover from. But despite the encouragement we gave to his grandmother to get him professional help, she kept saying, "He'll be all right. He's just finding his way."

Well, Matt did find his way one day. He found his way to a gun and used it to murder one of his classmates. The pain of rejection churning inside him came exploding out. A classmate had made fun of him in school, and after a physical altercation, Matt found him at a nearby park and shot him in the head.

At just sixteen years old, Matt was sentenced as an adult to life in prison without parole. Years earlier, his uncle received the exact same conviction. Although his grandmother said, "I never saw it coming," the signs had been there all along.

The emotional pressure of rejection causes some of us to *explode*. We externalize the trauma, punish *others* for our pain, and leave a trail of hurt people behind us. The pain of rejection is a ticking time bomb.

Maybe your rejection pain caused you to publicly berate a member of your work team because, after growing up in a home where you were pressured to perform, you can't handle criticism.

Maybe your rejection pain caused you to accuse your girl-friend of cheating with a man who said hello to her, simply because the first woman you loved left you for another guy.

Maybe your rejection pain caused you to curse out your mom for filing for divorce even though your dad was a serial cheater, because you are afraid of abandonment.

When you respond to rejection through *explosion*, you leave a trail of damaged people in your wake, just as Jocelyn and Matt did. But *implosion* can be an equally insidious expression of pain.

IMPLOSION

"I didn't know what to do," Sandy said.

After Matt was sentenced to life, she reached out to Big Brothers Big Sisters to thank her son's mentor for trying to help him. When she called our home looking for Tim, I spent forty-five minutes listening to her cry through tears of regret.

"I was young, homeless, prostituting myself. I couldn't take care of no baby. But I wanted to try. I stopped the drugs cold-turkey. I even told my pimp I needed to get off the streets so I could take care of my baby. When I looked at him that day he was born, I promised to do right by him.

.

And I did. For three whole months, I just stayed in the house and took care of him. But then . . ." Her voice trailed off as she began to cry.

"One of my friends showed up with some pills and told me she wanted to give 'em to me as a gift for my birthday. I left 'em on my nightstand for a week until, one day, I took 'em. I felt a rush and knew I was back hooked. I asked my neighbor if she could watch him for a few hours, but I ended up gone for two days," she cried.

"By the time my mom came and took him, I was so strung out I don't even know how long I was gone. When I went back to my apartment, they had thrown all my stuff away and somebody else was living there. I just went back to my old lifestyle. My pimp took me back but told me I had to work my way out of the debt I caused when I stopped tricking. I worked for nothin' but a sandwich a day for months."

My mind struggled to process what she was telling me.

"I'm so sorry to hear all of this, Sandy," I said. "It sounds like you needed as much help as Matt did."

Whereas Matt's rejection pain led him to *explode* and murder his classmate, Sandy's rejection from her father's abuse and mother's looking the other way caused her to *implode* into drug addiction and prostitution. She took her anguish out on herself, and Matt and his siblings became the collateral damage of her implosion. When we implode, we punish *ourselves* for our suffering.

Maybe your rejection pain caused you to implode into obesity, and now you're on the cusp of diabetes. You use food as a coping mechanism for being left out and overlooked your entire life.

Maybe your rejection pain caused you to implode into chronic exhaustion from being a workaholic. Achievement answers your dad's lifelong message of "you're not good enough."

Maybe your rejection pain caused you to implode into casual sex with people you barely know, because you can't imagine committing to someone who would break your heart again.

An explosive action identifies someone who needs help, but an implosion often goes undetected because it conceals self-harm. While explosive expressions such as physical aggression or verbal violence are seen as destructive, some implosive ones—addiction to fitness or hyperachievement—can be rewarded as virtuous.

I am no exception to this. Allow me to go first and tell you about me.

FROM PROBLEM TO PRODIGY

After my mom had Lee locked up for sexually abusing me, the police asked questions, and I told them as much detail as my six-year-old brain could manage. When we left the police station that day, I felt like everything was right in the world. But when Lee was nearing his prison release date, my mom told me to meet her out on the back patio of our home to talk.

"Nona, what would you think about Lee coming back?" she asked me.

Although I understood the question, I didn't understand the question. Why was she even asking?

"I . . . I don't want him to come back," I said, lowering my gaze to the ground.

I sensed the icy energy between us.

"Well, he's coming back," she said with finality. "I'm the adult, and I make the decisions."

With that, she got up and walked into the house, slamming the sliding glass door behind her. Just like Jesse did to David, she left me out in the field by myself.

The day she took me with her to pick up Lee from jail was the day I knew I didn't matter. The abuse resumed shortly after he moved back in, and since I had nowhere to turn, I started to explode in class. I became disruptive and talkative, earning my way to the principal's office as a regular guest.

But, one day in the fourth grade, my teacher pulled me aside and said something that changed the trajectory of my life: "Nona, you're so smart. You're a leader. I bet that if you tried, you could make all As in my class."

Up until that moment, my teachers had only ever called me a problem. When Ms. Johnson said those words to me, it was as if she hugged my little heart. She made me want to make her proud, so I did. I stopped being disruptive and started following her instructions. I did all my assignments and, lo and behold, I made all As in her class. But it didn't stop there.

I became super studious and ambitious. Nothing less than an A was sufficient. When I joined an extracurricular club or sports team, it wasn't enough for me to be a member or player. I had to be the president or captain. And I was. By the time I graduated from high school, I had passed enough advanced placement exams to start college as a first-year sophomore.

I was president of multiple student organizations, including my sorority. I made the dean's list and was on track to start medical school a year early until a divine intervention caused me to change my major.

By the time I was thirty-five, I had served in multiple high-profile executive roles, received countless statewide and national awards, recognitions, and board appointments, and received invitations to exclusive civic and social clubs. But as noted in the last chapter, while stars are *born* under pressure, stars can also *burn* under pressure.

A star implodes by consuming itself. I didn't have a support system to rely on as I worked myself crazy, so I just burned the candle of my energy from both ends. When I found myself crumbling beneath the pressure to perform, I had to ask the question *why?*

Why do I feel like nothing I achieve is enough?

Why do I feel like I need to achieve more to matter?

Why does the joy of achieving fade as soon as I achieve something?

Why does loneliness linger despite being surrounded by familiar faces?

Although I had gone from being a problem to a prodigy, I still felt a nagging sense that I wasn't enough. Instead of getting help, I imploded.

Between the ages of twenty-one and thirty, I gained almost one hundred pounds from eating sweets and fatty foods. I would stay up late working and wake up early to work some more. I saw myself as a failure if someone else won a prestigious award instead of me. In the back of my mind, I believed I deserved the pain.

When we're wrestling with the pain of rejection, we tend to look inward and arrive at the conclusion that something is wrong with us. But what if, instead of either exploding or imploding, we pursue a third way—*up*loading? What if we train our eyes in a different direction? Instead of looking inward, we can train ourselves to look upward.

When the gift of rejection lands on our doorstep, the pain it comes wrapped in can make us want to write "return to sender" on it. But if we look upward and allow God to help us learn from it, he can make us *better* because of it.

RECALL

- There is nothing you can accumulate around you that will fill a deficit within you.
- The pain of rejection molds us like clay.
- Bitterness is an instant replay of the events that hurt us.
- Hurt within us can hurt other people.
- The pain of rejection within us often works its way out of us.
- The pain of rejection is a ticking time bomb.
- When we internalize the pain of rejection, it causes us to implode.

RECEIVE

Brothers and sisters, I do not consider myself yet to have taken hold of it. But one thing I do: Forgetting what is behind and straining toward what is ahead, I press on toward the goal to win the prize for which God has called me heavenward in Christ Jesus. (Philippians 3:13–14)

RECITE

Lord, help me identify how rejection has been expressing itself in my life. Help me admit where I have fallen short of your grace. Help me see how I've hurt others and myself. My desire is to honor you with my thoughts, actions, and intentions, so give me the grace to acknowledge how I have failed because of unaddressed rejection.

REFLECT

Take a moment to think about and answer the following questions:

1. How has the pain of rejection led to bad habits?
2. Do you find yourself exploding or imploding, and how so?
3. What would it take for you to begin inviting God into your pain instead of trying to figure it out on your own?

CHAPTER

FROM BITTER TO BETTER

"That was *incredible*," my host said as she walked me to the car. "Wow. What a night. We have to have you back again soon!"

I smiled wide and hugged her, then climbed into the black Cadillac Escalade for the drive to the airport.

As my plane reached cruising altitude, I felt both exhausted and grateful for what God had enabled that night. I had been the closing speaker for a conference of three thousand attendees. The altar had filled with men, women, and young people in tears, responding to the move of the Holy Spirit.

Earlier that day, I had felt unprepared for the event. Between my workload, family responsibilities, and church commitments, I didn't have much time to get ready.

Before heading to the event, I had slipped a pillow off the hotel bed, knelt on it on the floor, and prayed, "God, I don't have to tell you how unprepared I feel. You know. But I surrender myself for your purpose. I don't feel worthy of standing before your sons and daughters as your representative, but you are holy, sovereign, and full of mercy. I lay down everything I think I know so that you can stand tall within me. I leave any insecurity at the foot of the cross because this moment isn't about me. It's about you. Be glorified through me, Father."

It was the prayer I pray every time I speak—the one that has readied me to be God's instrument at that conference and many others.

When I started to receive speaking invitations, I had no idea what I was doing. I wanted *so* badly to have someone take me under their wing and mentor me, like the apostle Paul did with Timothy.

During that time, I attended a national gathering for Christian influencers under the age of forty. Over dinner one night, they *all* shared how an older, prominent speaker or pastor had become a spiritual parent to them.

They told stories of vacationing with their mentor and being invited to speak at their large conferences and events. Several people even said a spiritual parent was bankrolling family travel costs to ensure ministry didn't separate the speaker from their spouse and kids.

I was amazed and sad. I knew these people. I saw them at conferences and events, and we had each other's phone numbers, but none of them had ever offered to mentor me.

That's when the rejection talk track started playing.

Nona, why would anyone want to be your spiritual mother when your birth mother doesn't even want you?

You don't have millions of followers like they do, Nona, so why would anyone waste their time on you?

Who do you think you are? Why would they invest in you when they can invest in someone more famous than you?

I wore a smile on my face as I listened to the incredible ways their spiritual parents had supported and accelerated their ministries, but deep down inside, my heart broke. I felt rejected because others had been accepted.

As they traded story after story, I felt more and more isolated. I felt more and more alone. I felt left out in the field of ministry by myself. Although I masked my pain through laughter, after dinner was over, I went back to my hotel room and sat on the edge of my bed in silence. I felt a familiar wave of bitterness come over me, so I turned my attention to the only one I knew to turn to.

"God, you know how much I've wanted to have a spiritual mother adopt me and teach me about ministry. You know how much I've wanted to have someone open doors for me. But you've hidden me in plain sight. It's as if these women see me but *don't* see me! Why?"

"Before I answer you," I heard the Lord say, "why do you believe you need a spiritual mother?"

"Because I don't know what I'm doing. I need someone to guide me."

"Why do you believe you don't know what you're doing?"

"I've never been to seminary. I don't have any advanced degrees in theology. I'm in way over my head!"

"Which seminary did Peter attend?"

"I mean, they didn't have seminaries then."

"Really? How do you think Paul was a Pharisee of Pharisees?"

"I'm just saying I don't feel like I have credibility."

"So you believe being accepted by a spiritual mother would give you credibility?"

"Yes."

"When you're invited to speak, do they ask for an endorsement letter from a prominent speaker?"

"Well, no, but . . ."

"So where did this idea come from?"

As I surrendered to the silence, my mind flooded with memories of times when my birth mother rejected me. Times when friends and lovers rejected me. Times when I was overlooked for opportunities and recognitions. And that's when the source of my longing became clear. I didn't want *credibility*. I wanted to be *wanted* and *accepted*. I wanted someone who mattered to *me* to say I mattered to *them* so that *I* would finally matter.

"Nona, I use the least likely people for my purposes because I don't share credit for miracles. If you had the endorsement of a world-renowned speaker, you might thank *them* for the doors their reputation opened for you, but because you don't, you have no one to thank but *me*. I didn't choose you because *everyone else* chose you, Nona. I chose you *because* they *didn't*."

Tears formed in my eyes as I received God's revelation. It opened a dam, and just when I thought I had cried as much as I could, I heard the Lord ask, "Why do you need someone else? Why am I not enough for you?"

I felt a gut punch. I had been seeking validation from everyone *except* the One who had already offered it—the only One who truly mattered. While searching for the approval of an earthly mother, I had devalued the approval of my heavenly Father. God had single-handedly been the spiritual parent I so desperately wanted and needed, but I had discounted his divine orchestration.

The pain of rejection made me focus on who walked away instead of who never left.

In Hebrews 13:5 (NKJV) God says, "I will never leave you nor forsake you." When we *leave* someone, we *physically* remove ourselves. When we *forsake* someone, we *emotionally* withdraw from them. In this verse, we are reminded that God will never do either. He promises to stay close to us, both physically and emotionally. When others walk away or ostracize us, God remains.

In Romans 5:6–8, the apostle Paul writes, "At just the right time, when we were still powerless, Christ died for the ungodly. Very rarely will anyone die for a righteous person, though for a good person someone might possibly dare to die. But God demonstrates his own love for us in this: While we were still sinners, Christ died for us." While *we* often reject God, he loves and accepts *us*.

When I reflect on my journey, I realize that the entire time I was yearning for someone on earth to accept me, my Father in heaven had been doing it.

Even when I didn't recognize it.

Even when I was ungrateful for it.

Even when I took it for granted.

Every rejection I've experienced at the hands of others pales in comparison to God's overwhelming love for me. But my bitterness sometimes prevents me from seeing it.

I imagine you've faced similar challenges.

Maybe your mom kicked you out when you got pregnant in high school, but you graduated from college and now own the home you raise your daughter in. Though God's protection covered you, you still carry bitterness toward your mom.

Or maybe you launched a business after your manager overlooked you for a promotion, and now you make more money than you would have at your previous job. Though God's favor covered you, you still carry bitterness toward your old boss.

Or maybe your husband of seventeen years left you, but being single has reintroduced you to old hopes and dreams, and you're seeing the world he never wanted to see. Although God's grace covered you, you still carry bitterness toward your ex-husband.

Pausing to reflect on God's goodness in our lives despite our pain helps us see that he is in control, not our offenders.

In 1 Corinthians 1:27, Paul writes, "God chose the foolish things of the world to shame the wise; God chose the weak things of the world to shame the strong." I am a living testament to that truth. If you take time to open the gift of your rejection, you might realize that you are too.

When you learn to receive rejection as a gift, you will understand that even people's rejection of you can serve God's purpose for you.

THE OPEN FRAMEWORK

No matter how long you've been alive and how many Bible verses you know about God's love, rejection still hurts. So how exactly do we find purpose in it? Enter the OPEN framework.

OPEN stands for observe, pray, explore, and name. Over the years, I've honed this practice while wrestling with rejection. The four steps have helped me better process my pain.

They've also helped me remember past rejections with less emotional sting.

You too can use OPEN to harness your pain and propel your purpose. In the following chapters, I will use this framework to help you work through the four gifts of rejection.

Observe

Rejection can flood you with thoughts and feelings. But before you allow them to drown you in discouragement, take a moment to ask, "What am I thinking and feeling right now?"

Find a piece of paper or open a notes app and jot down your thoughts. As you review them, take the process a step further by asking yourself, "Is this thought true?" You might also name the main emotion gripping your heart. Is it anger? Fear? Sadness?

Maybe you didn't get invited to an event you were looking forward to, so you think, "I never get invited to anything! Nobody wants me around." You feel a mixture of anger and sadness, but when you take time to consider these statements, you realize they aren't true. Not only have you been invited to other events, but a friend you haven't spoken to in months has been asking you out to lunch and you haven't made the time.

Maybe you weren't selected for the store manager job you applied for, so you think, "I'm not smart enough. I'll never get ahead." You feel deflated and hopeless, but when you take time to consider these statements, you realize they aren't true. Not only are you the person who figured out a complex point-of-sale system, you have also risen from the ranks of stock clerk to assistant store manager faster than usual.

Maybe your estranged mother spreads yet another lie

about you, leading cousins, aunts, and uncles to shun you. You think, "I have no family. I'm all alone." You feel attacked and vulnerable, but when you take time to consider these statements, you realize they aren't true. Not only does your favorite aunt call you to say how much she loves you, but one of your cousins stopped by with dinner and a board game to take your mind off the situation.

Instead of catastrophizing, try to assess your thoughts and feelings as an impartial observer. Identify the lies, then take the next step: pray.

Pray

When I feel the pain of rejection, I often want the person who rejected me to feel as much pain as I do. I want them to know what it's like to be on the receiving end of their actions.

I know I'm not the only one. Have you ever found yourself typing a "hot" text that rushes out of your fingers with hostility?

Or have you found yourself making a "hot" phone call, where your heart is beating so hard it makes your temples pulsate?

Or have you found yourself starting a "hot" meeting, where you barge into your coworker's cubicle before you've gathered your thoughts?

Before you send that text, make that phone call, or step into that office, pause and pray. Ask God to show you *why* you have those thoughts and feelings. Why are they allowed to live rent-free in your heart and mind?

When you were left out of the event, why did you think,

"I never get invited to anything! Nobody wants me around"? What belief about yourself made you rush to that conclusion?

When your manager denied your promotion, why did you think, "I'm not smart enough. I'll never get ahead"? What belief about yourself made you rush to that conclusion?

When your mother spread lies about you, why did you think, "I have no family. I'm all alone"? What belief about yourself made you rush to that conclusion?

In Ephesians 4:26–27 (NKJV), Paul writes, "'Be angry, and do not sin': do not let the sun go down on your wrath, nor give place to the devil." The word *place* comes from the Greek *topos*, which means opportunity, power, or occasion for acting. When we react to rejection with anger and hostility, we give the devil opportunity, power, and occasion for acting. These conditions allow strongholds to form.

A stronghold is a fortified thought pattern that results from ruminating on it. Once it begins to form, you become vulnerable to spiritual attack. Asking "Why am I feeling this way and thinking these thoughts?" will help you identify the mental and emotional strongholds in your life.

You need God's supernatural power to break those bonds. The conclusion of each chapter includes a "Recite" section for this very purpose. When you submit to God's power and presence, freedom is sure to follow. Why? Because when the Son sets you free, you are truly free indeed (John 8:36)!

Explore

Every rejection contains the gift of insight into yourself and others. So dig a bit deeper to explore what your rejection experience has given you.

For example, when you weren't invited to that event, you realized how much you desire social connection with others. Your hurt uncovered an insight that you can immediately apply: be a friend to make a friend.

Every rejection contains the gift of insight into yourself and others.

By embracing this lesson, you can shift from a passive posture of "rejection victim" to an active posture of "change agent," making a conscious choice to use what you've learned about yourself to change your future.

<u>N</u>ame

Only the power of God gives purpose to rejection, but we must partner with him in that work. Your newfound insights will serve as a gift only if you set a clear action plan for how to incorporate them in your life. To do this well, you need to *name your next step.*

In the case of not getting invited to the event, the explore step helped you realize that social connection is important to you. Now you can put that insight to work by reaching out to the friend who wants to have lunch. You can also decide to move on from the host who rejected you *or* befriend her and build a relationship.

Either way, you need to name the next step and restore your agency in the situation.

The OPEN framework helps you receive the gift in each rejection, so now let's explore the four steps in more detail.

RECALL

- We can feel rejected when others are accepted.
- The pain of rejection can make you focus on who walked away instead of who never left.
- While *we* often reject God, he loves and accepts *us*.
- Instead of looking inward, we can train ourselves to look upward.
- The OPEN framework equips you to harness your pain and propel your purpose.

RECEIVE

Though my father and mother forsake me,
  the LORD will receive me. (Psalm 27:10)

RECITE

Lord, help me see your handiwork in my pain. Remind me of your goodness when all I feel is hurt. Give me the grace to surrender to what is instead of being consumed by what could have been. I want to be made better by the experiences that have left me broken, but I don't know where to start. I take comfort in knowing that you do. Thank you for being true to your word. Even when I don't feel you near me, I know you have never left me.

REFLECT

Take a moment to think about and answer the following questions:

1. How has rejection left you bitter, and how does that bitterness display itself in your life?
2. Who has been a consistent source of support in your life, and how can you spend more time with that person?
3. Which part of the OPEN framework will be most difficult for you to consistently implement, and why?

PART 3

UNWRAPPING
THE GIFT

INTRODUCTION

A Field of Gifts

We have covered a lot of ground over the last six chapters, and my hope is that you are entering this final part of the book with a higher level of self-awareness, which will help you OPEN the four gifts we will examine over the remaining chapters.

So what are those gifts?

When we first met David in 1 Samuel 16:5–11, he was the nameless, youngest son of Jesse who had been left out in a field tending sheep by himself while his father and brothers met with the prophet Samuel. Although initially a place where David was discarded, the field became the training ground where his courage and confidence *in God* was forged. And that divine courage and confidence led him to challenge Goliath when no one else would. His victory happened not *in spite of* being rejected but *because of* it. God honored David's suffering and then used it to prepare him for his ultimate assignment as king of Israel.

Looking closely at David's story can help us understand the four gifts of rejection.

#1: The gift of rejection positions you for purpose.

When I was in high school, I started planning to become an oncologist. I wanted so badly to cure the disease that took my father. While my classmates were taking electives like art and physical education, I was studying physics, biology, and physiology. When I graduated, I enrolled at the University of Florida as a microbiology and cell-science major, and my grades had me on track to start medical school my fourth year of undergrad.

During the summer between my second and third year of college, I did research with the National Institutes of Health. My project sponsor was an older physician who was jaded, gruff, and mean. But his colleagues still highly respected him for his scholarly work.

One day, after I'd given him an update on my project, he asked me, "Why do you want to be a doctor?"

I responded with bright eyes and enthusiasm, "I want to give people hope and be a partner in their healthcare."

His thick, gray eyebrows furrowed as he frowned and barked, "Doctors don't give people hope! We just tell the facts. This isn't about hope. It's about science! You're not cut out to be a doctor, kid."

I felt so defeated by his words and tone that when I made it back to my dorm that night, I decided to change my major to communications.

I felt like a failure before I had even started. When he looked at me, he saw nothing more than incompetent idealism personified. Forget that I got into the program because I had a 4.0 GPA. My desire to give people hope apparently disqualified me in his mind. That experience changed the trajectory of my life and career—and hindsight has made me so grateful it did.

If I had gone to medical school and become the oncologist I had intended to be, it's highly unlikely that I would be writing this book. It's highly unlikely that I would be preaching and speaking around the world. It's highly unlikely that my life would look anything like it does. And this is why when you OPEN the gift of rejection, you realize it positions you for purpose.

As much as I still love science, math, and medicine, I would never have imagined how deeply I would love what I get to do right now. As painful as it was in the moment and as heartbroken as I felt at the time, I can see how that doctor's *dis*couragement was actually the *en*couragement needed to redirect me to where I am today. Which raises questions for you:

What does *not* getting that job make room for you to do?

What does *not* keeping that relationship create time for you to do?

What does *not* being selected allow you to try instead?

The gift of rejection positions you for purpose. Instead of lamenting what you lost, begin to ask God, "What are you positioning me for?"

The gift of rejection positions you for purpose.

#2: The gift of rejection reveals people's role in your destiny.

I believe relationships have one of three durations in our lives: a reason, a season, or a lifetime. When a relationship happens for a reason, once the reason is fulfilled, the relationship dissolves.

Let's say in your job you are placed on a cross-functional team. You work in HR, another person works in finance, and another person works in marketing. The goal of your team is to reduce the electricity bill for your building. After meeting together a few times, you come up with a recommendation and present it to the company president, who approves it. After the presentation, your team dissolves because you achieved your purpose. No hard feelings, right? Would you feel rejected because the others on the team no longer contacted you? Probably not.

Lifetime relationships are exactly what the word means. For *life*. These are the people we have a deep connection with, whether by birth (i.e., parents, siblings, and extended family) or by choice (best friends). While reason and lifetime relationships are pretty straightforward, things can get a bit complicated in seasonal relationships.

A seasonal relationship ends when the conditions it exists under change. For example, when my boys were in preschool, they had a few friends that I would schedule playdates with. While they were playing with their friends, I would make small talk with their friends' moms. As my boys grew older and they moved to a different school, I no longer spoke with those moms because the conditions under which the relationship existed changed. My boys were in a different school and had a different set of friends. I didn't feel rejected because those moms didn't contact me, and I'm pretty sure they felt the same because the relationship was seasonal.

Although we tend to assume that our birth relationships (i.e., parents, siblings, and extended family) and special friendships are lifetime relationships, they can sometimes be seasonal. And this is where the pain of rejection can become especially hard. Since rejection requires first believing we are accepted, when a relationship we *thought* would be for a lifetime proves only to be seasonal, that can leave us feeling wounded.

We can't always control when or if a relationship season ends. In fact, trying to make seasonal relationships become lifetime relationships is like trying to keep a snowball from winter through spring and summer. It doesn't work. That doesn't necessarily mean something is wrong with you; it just means that the season of that person's role in your life has ended. Instead of trying to make someone stay in your life when their time is up, you will learn in chapter 8 how to let them go so you can embrace what God wants to do in your future.

The gift of rejection reveals people's role in your destiny.

The gift of rejection reveals people's role in your destiny.

#3: The gift of rejection anchors your identity.

Have you ever wanted to keep someone in your life so badly that you changed yourself to better fit their desires? Maybe you wore your hair a certain way or dressed a certain way or voted a certain way or watched certain programs or ate certain food, all with the goal of making that person happy.

Or maybe you majored in engineering because your parents believed that the only way to be successful was to become an engineer. As you sent out applications for engineering jobs, you secretly hoped you wouldn't get an interview so you could pursue your true passion for making hip-hop beats.

Or maybe you ran track in high school, not because you liked the sport but because you wanted to fit in with a certain group of kids who ran track.

I am especially sensitive to this because I'm a mother of two sons. I have watched them work hard to fit in with a certain friend group, only to get discarded anyway. After they changed their personalities to better fit in and changed the way they talked to better fit in, I would still end up wiping tears from their confused eyes as they wrestled with being rejected despite "checking the boxes" they thought would lead to acceptance.

I bet you know what this is like too. Someone's rejection of you after you've done everything to meet their expectations can leave you feeling like something is fundamentally wrong with you. And because of this, rejection can cause you to become a bit of a shape-shifter—someone whose likes and interests shift based on whoever you are seeking approval from. But if you take a step back and soberly see the situation for what it is, you will realize that people who accept you only when you are who they want you to be aren't actually accepting "you." They are accepting themselves as mirrored by you.

The one and only consistent source of approval you will

ever receive in this world is from God. And because of this, the gift of rejection teaches us to live our lives to please him and him alone. We will explore this more in chapter 9 by taking a closer look at how David's life illustrates this for us. *The gift of rejection anchors your identity.*

The gift of rejection anchors your identity.

#4: The gift of rejection draws you nearer to God.

When we experience rejection, we tend to react in one of three ways: fight, flight, or freeze. When we fight, we meet the pain of rejection with hostility, lashing out in anger at the source of our rejection. When we flee, we create distance between ourselves and the source of our rejection, maybe avoiding interactions with them or refusing to have any contact. When we freeze, we allow the fear of more pain to paralyze us into inaction.

So what do *you* do when you are stinging from the pain of rejection?

Do you call your best friend to tell them about it?

Do you pull out your journal to write about it?

Do you go on social media and make a post about it?

Some people turn to addictions when nursing the pain of rejection: alcohol, drugs, infidelity, pornography, etc.

Chapter 10 will encourage you to take a different path: turn to God. He is the only one who can truly satisfy. I believe we miss God's hand in our lives because we aren't looking for it. We don't feel God's presence in our lives because we aren't pursuing it. But when you allow the gift of rejection to draw you nearer to God, you realize that when everyone else forsakes you, his promise never to leave you or forsake you stands true. David was able to fight Goliath because he could point to the protection God had repeatedly provided for him when he was left out in the field tending the flock by himself.

When I was devastated by the pain of my mother's words, God protected me.

When I was broken by the pain of Barry cheating on me, God protected me.

When I was undermined by colleagues who were jealous of me, God protected me.

God protected me because I turned to him and allowed my pain to draw me close to his presence. Because of this, I experienced peace in the midst of confusion, joy in the midst of sorrow, love in the midst of fear. And this is what David's life teaches us time and time again.

The gift of rejection draws you nearer to God. *The gift of rejection draws you nearer to God.* So now let's start to OPEN the gifts of your rejection.

RECALL

- The gift of rejection positions you for purpose.
- The gift of rejection reveals people's role in your destiny.
- The gift of rejection anchors your identity.
- The gift of rejection draws you nearer to God.

CHAPTER

GIFT #1

Positioning You for Purpose

I was less than six months into a new leadership role at a large global company when a member of the communications team asked me to speak about my team's work at an internal company event. After it was over, he emailed me and said I did a great job and asked if I was willing to speak at external events too. I was honored and enthusiastically agreed. Soon I found myself in several meetings getting trained as a company spokesperson.

Although I had not been hired as a spokesperson, our company was invited to have a speaking role at so many conferences that the communications team built an internal speakers bureau of leaders to send out on behalf of the company. Given my passion for our mission, I couldn't wait to help share it with others.

My first external event was in Miami. It was the largest gathering in the United States of Hispanic and Latino professionals in the entertainment industry. We were an event sponsor and had a slot for a twenty-minute talk about our company's commitment to diversity. When I reviewed the talking points the communications team prepared, I felt they were too sterile and asked if I could make some tweaks. "I want to tell my story. I want to make the mission personal to me and my journey. Can I rewrite this and get your thoughts?" I asked Tom, my communications team counterpart.

"We don't normally let execs go off script or even massage talking points too much, but I'll take a look at what you put together. Can you send me your rewrite by tomorrow and I'll run it by my team for their feedback?"

Shortly after I sent my rewrite, Tom texted me and told me he loved my changes. His team agreed, and a couple of weeks later, we all made our way to Miami for the event. The event room was filled with a couple thousand people clearly enjoying themselves while eating lunch. When I took the stage, there was so much loud talking and uproarious laughter that I wasn't sure people would be able to hear what I had to say or pay attention even if they could. But I started to tell my story.

I shared how the person I had become was statistically improbable. I shared the many ways that sexual abuse, physical abuse, and abandonment should have derailed my life and sent me down a path of failure. Then I shared about the life-changing power of community. How my community of teachers and pastors encouraged me. How they looked beyond my poor behavior and believed in my potential. How, because of community, I had become the unlikely exception to the rule. I connected our mission of giving people the power to build community with enabling people around the world to find belonging and hope.

After I stepped off the stage, one of the women who had been serving lunch walked up with tears in her eyes and said, "I had to stop serving because I couldn't hold back the tears as you spoke. Your story is my story too." After I gave her a big hug, one of the male executives from a major Spanish-language media company came up with tears in his eyes and said, "That happened to me too. I've never told anyone." I spent more time speaking with people on the floor than I spent speaking from the stage, and when my communications colleagues saw the response to my talk, they grabbed me afterward and said, "Nona, this is just the beginning. We need you speaking on behalf of the company everywhere, every day!"

When they gave similarly glowing feedback to my manager, Diane, she told me she was proud of how I was representing the team and the company. Over the following months, they booked me for countless media interviews and speaking events. Despite the travel, I made sure I was able to join weekly one-on-one meetings with Diane as well as team meetings with my peers and direct reports. I made it my priority to do an excellent job in what I had been hired to do, because the speaking opportunities were the cherry on top of the sundae, not the sundae.

When performance evaluation season came around, I submitted my thoughts on my performance across all dimensions of my role, including serving as a company spokesperson. When the performance review letter landed in my inbox, it said I received an "exceeds expectations" rating. I was so excited and smiled from ear to ear.

But when meeting day arrived, Diane dropped a bomb in my lap. "Your rating is an 'exceeds,' Nona," she said. "But I need you to focus on your core work. I feel like all the media and speaking has become a distraction. You're not doing any more interviews or conferences."

I tried to stifle my shock to keep it from fully blooming across my face. "Is something wrong?" I asked. "Is there something else you need me to do that I'm not doing?"

"No, nothing is specifically wrong. I just think . . . I think all the speaking is a distraction. I'm not approving any more trips."

Although the gears of my mind were spinning out of control, I plastered a smile on my face and nodded and said, "Okay." I don't remember what she said the rest of the meeting. Her decision knocked the wind out of my sails. After the meeting, I reached out to Tom to tell him the news.

"Yeah, I know," he said. "My manager told me this morning. We're all confused. You're one of the best spokespeople we have. It just doesn't make sense."

I was good friends with Tom's manager, Angelica, so I asked her if she had any more context for Diane's decision.

She asked to grab lunch to talk. When we sat down, she said, "So, real deal, Nona?"

"Yes, that's what I want. What's going on?"

"She's jealous. She told me that *she* should be speaking on behalf of the company, not you."

"I never asked to do it in the first place! And she encouraged it! I'm so confused right now," I said.

"Well, that was before people started to invite you to cover events she wants to speak at. Word of advice: just lay low. She won't be here forever."

Although Angelica was trying to encourage me, I was

heartbroken that Diane had the power to unilaterally close a door when I was serving the company well. I felt the familiar pain of rejection churning in my heart as I sat there feeling discarded.

Do you know how that feels? Maybe you spent the last three years conducting research for your doctoral dissertation and felt confident heading into your defense, only to have one member of the committee decide it wasn't good enough. You watched your years of work go up in flames and left the presentation feeling discarded and rejected.

Or maybe you planned and hosted fundraisers all year for your children's school in hopes of being elected president of the PTA, but when it came time for the vote, a mom whose husband coached the local college football team was chosen instead of you even though she never volunteered during the year. You watched the hours you gave go up in flames and left the meeting feeling discarded and rejected.

Perhaps you got a job to help pay your husband's way through law school because you both agreed you would sacrifice first so he could fund your law-school tuition later. A few years after he landed a good job, he said he didn't feel comfortable putting your young children in daycare and didn't support you going to law school. You watched years of sacrifice go up in flames and left the conversation feeling discarded and rejected.

Although the *pain* of rejection can leave us feeling discarded in the moment, the *gift* of rejection teaches us that, in God's hands, closed doors simply redirect us toward his good and perfect will. In God's hands, rejection positions you for purpose.

In God's hands, rejection positions you for purpose.

ACCESS GRANTED

When I first started working for the company formerly known as Facebook, I learned that a large church leadership conference was hosting a learning track focused on technology. I saw it as an opportunity to share best practices for leveraging the Facebook family of apps for ministry, so I got in touch with the host to pitch the idea. "Thank you so much for taking my call, Tanner. I would love to find a way to share at your conference."

"How much money are you planning to pay to sponsor?" he asked.

"We're in the middle of our fiscal year, so I don't have any discretionary dollars this year. I think the information will be valuable, though. I get so many questions from pastors that it's a bit overwhelming."

"Let's talk when you have sponsorship dollars. I don't platform companies without that."

I left the conversation feeling deflated. My inbox was full of questions from church leaders around the world who were desperately trying to use Facebook for ministry, but they were confused and overwhelmed. I thought it was the perfect opportunity to answer questions in mass with a workshop. Instead, the conference host reduced my value down to a dollar sign and rejected me based on his view that I wasn't worth the opportunity cost.

When a person with a platform or power or notoriety rejects us, it can feel like the only door we had got shut and padlocked in our face. But when we're in the will of

God, though they may close a door, God will open a window. Though they may close the window, God will knock down a wall. I believe God smiles in the face of people's rejection of us. *People's rejection proves God's power.*

People's rejection proves God's power.

After Samuel anointed David as king, and before he had met Goliath, the Bible says in 1 Samuel 16:14, "Now the Spirit of the LORD had departed from Saul, and an evil spirit from the LORD tormented him."

As a reminder, Saul was the first man anointed king of Israel. He had been chosen by God, not elected by the people. Once God anointed David to be the next king, the Spirit of the Lord that had rested on Saul departed from him and was replaced by an evil spirit to torment him. The evil spirit was punishment for Saul's disobedience to God (1 Samuel 15:1–9).

> Saul's attendants said to him, "See, an evil spirit from God is tormenting you. Let our lord command his servants here to search for someone who can play the lyre. He will play when the evil spirit from God comes on you, and you will feel better. (1 Samuel 16:15–16)

A lyre was a stringed instrument that was played softly and was believed to have therapeutic effects for its listener.

> So Saul said to his attendants, "Find someone who plays well and bring him to me."
> One of the servants answered, "I have seen a son of Jesse of Bethlehem who knows how to play the lyre. He is

a brave man and a warrior. He speaks well and is a fine-looking man. And the LORD is with him."

Then Saul sent messengers to Jesse and said, "Send me your son David, who is with the sheep." (1 Samuel 16:17–19)

David wasn't physically in the room, but a person in the room brought David's name into it. Not only did God give David access to a room he wasn't physically present in, but when the king went to find David, guess where he found him. In a field. Tending sheep. By himself. The king found him in the same place David had been relegated to over and over, day after day, month after month, year after year. And because David was always in that place of rejection, the servant knew exactly where to find him.

Rejection positions you to be found by people who will be looking for you.

Maybe your ex-husband walked away from you and left you single and hurting. But your current husband has too much integrity to have ever approached you when you were married. By abandoning you, your ex left you in the field of singleness, where the man of your dreams found you!

Or perhaps the employer you worked yourself to the point of exhaustion for thanked you with a layoff notice. But because of the excellent work you did with external vendors, the moment you shared the news on LinkedIn, several vendors reached out with offers of a higher salary. By laying you off, your former employer left you in the field of unemployment, where the nonsolicitation clause that prevented the vendors from recruiting you was nullified!

Although you may feel forgotten or lost, God knows *exactly* where you are. No matter what access you believe you were denied, God holds the master key.

About a year after Tanner denied my request to speak at his conference, he called me out of the blue. "Hi, Nona. Thanks for taking my call."

"Of course, Tanner. How can I help?"

"Well, I have to first apologize. When you called me last year, I didn't realize who you were or what you did. I'm planning a large women's leadership conference, and I was sharing the vision with a friend of mine when he brought up your name as the perfect person to speak at it. I was just wondering if you would be willing?"

I felt like I was in a twilight zone as I listened to him. Not only did he invite me to speak at his conference, but whereas he originally asked me what I was willing to pay *him* to speak, after the endorsement of his friend, he was offering to pay *me* to speak. *God will place your name in rooms that you don't have access to.*

TO DIANE, WITH LOVE

After my lunch with Angelica where she shared that Diane had shut down my corporate speaking because of jealousy, I took her advice and kept my head down and worked. I enjoyed my work, so I wasn't disappointed in the job. I was disappointed that Diane had punished me for doing my job *well*.

Although the communications team had previously handled all my speaking invitations, I received an email in my inbox one day from someone asking me to speak at their upcoming church conference. I immediately replied to the email and explained that I wasn't able to speak on behalf of the company at that time. The email they sent next would forever shift the trajectory of my life: "No worries, Nona. Can you just speak as yourself? Our invitation is specific to you, so not necessarily the company. Would that work?"

I was momentarily stunned. It had never occurred to me that someone would want me to speak as *just* myself. I forwarded the email to Tom and asked for his guidance. "I don't see any problem with it, Nona. As long as they don't promote your job title or say you're speaking for the company, it's fine with me!"

I responded to the person with an acceptance, and three Saturdays later I stood on a stage in Nashville, Tennessee, speaking as myself about my assigned topic. After the event, James, the host, handed me an envelope that contained a check. I told him I couldn't accept compensation. He looked puzzled and asked why.

"Well, this is part of my salaried work, so I can't receive outside compensation."

"That's odd, Nona," he said. "Why would you not be able to get paid for something you're doing on your own time? You're not speaking for the company, right?"

His question swirled through my thoughts. "Hmm. Good

question, James," I said. "I hadn't thought about that, actually. Let me ask a couple people internally."

I took the check and placed it in my backpack, and once en route to the airport, I emailed Tom and asked how I should handle the check. He emailed to say, "That's your decision, Nona. Compensation is only prohibited when you speak on behalf of the company since it would be part of your job. Other than that, it's your time, so it's your money."

I was floored. The host had already paid for my airfare, lodging, and ground transportation. I opened the envelope and pulled out the check. It was for $1,000! The most I had ever been paid before that was $100 to preach at a local church conference, which I thought was generous because it allowed my husband and me to go out to dinner. I was suddenly confronted with the unexpected reality that when Diane closed the door for me to speak on behalf of the company, a new door had opened for me to speak on behalf of myself.

After that event, more people invited me to speak at their events. I didn't expect compensation or have a set fee. So sometimes I got airfare and a hotel, and sometimes I got airfare, hotel, and an honorarium. But after almost a year of speaking at more and more events on the weekends and evenings, my friend Jeremy lovingly pulled my coattail for a heart-to-heart. "Nona, this is unsustainable. I see you speaking everywhere all the time. Are you taking care of yourself? How is your family?"

"I know. I'm exhausted, but I feel bad saying no. My family is okay right now, but I know I can't keep this up long-term."

"Have you ever thought about putting the information you're sharing into a book? At least that way you can point people to a resource instead of having to travel everywhere."

"That's a good idea, actually. Maybe I can make a playbook or resource guide and share it with people for free. I can make it downloadable on my website too."

"People will pay good money for what you're sharing, Nona. Don't be so quick to give it away for free. By the way, how much are you charging for speaking?"

"Charging? Nothing. Who am I to charge anybody?" I said with a laugh.

"Are you kidding? You're literally speaking at every conference I'm at. You should be compensated for what you're doing. You need to set a fee."

"A fee? What would that even be? I wouldn't know what to charge."

"I can give you some ideas. I know how much some people charge because I'm the one booking them for many of the conferences you're speaking at. And, trust me, the cost of being away from your family is higher than anything you're being paid. Especially if you're doing it for free."

That night, Jeremy helped me map out a fee schedule for the first time. I couldn't believe anyone would pay real money for me to speak at an event, but after a lot of encouragement, I realized the value in what Jeremy was saying. The next time an invitation landed in my inbox, I shared my fee and the host readily accepted. I was amazed.

Within eight months of establishing my fee schedule, I was making as much from speaking fees as I was from my corporate salary. And I was doing it *while* working my full-time job—all because Diane had closed the door on letting me speak for *free*.

Thank you, Diane. Thank you for being an instrument of rejection.

When I opened the gift of her rejection, I realized that her decision did not harm me; it positioned me. Although I enjoyed speaking for the company, I never thought of myself as a speaker per se. It wasn't until Diane forced me to the sidelines that I learned how God uses rejection for our good. *God uses rejection to unleash purpose.*

God uses rejection to unleash purpose.

POSITIONED FOR GROWTH

I invest a lot of time and energy into personal development. I have read hundreds of books and articles on leadership to strengthen my character, and I've also attended conferences and workshops to sharpen my management skills. But when I reflect on my growth, it was opening the gift of rejection and allowing it to teach me that helped me grow *the most*.

The gift of being rejected by my mother taught me to stay focused in school despite feeling unloved and unwanted at home.

The gift of being rejected by Barry taught me that people don't do what they do because of me; they do what they do because of them.

The gift of being rejected by my manager taught me that closed doors are simply God's detour signs.

When we pray and ask God to help us grow in our character, skills, or abilities, what we are actually doing is asking God to put us to the test. James 1:2–4 says, "Consider it pure joy, my brothers and sisters, whenever you face trials of many kinds, because you know that the testing of your faith produces perseverance. Let perseverance finish its work so that you may be mature and complete, not lacking anything."

Growth is not downloaded from "on high" simply because we pray for it. Growth is the fruit of maturing in the face of adversity.

Growth is the fruit of maturing in the face of adversity.

After Diane put the kibosh on my corporate speaking, I initially felt resentful and discouraged, but instead of yielding to those emotions and allowing them to consume me, I decided to use the experience as a springboard to personal growth. I went to God in prayer and honestly shared how I was feeling. Instead of denying my anger and pain, I simply admitted it and asked God to give me the wisdom to receive whatever lesson he wanted to teach me. I asked him to give me the grace to serve Diane and my team with excellence, even though my heart was still tender from her rejection.

I spent the next year fully leaning into my work and my team. I led several large-scale initiatives on behalf of Diane, and my work gained a lot of internal visibility at the highest levels of the company. I was invited to join meetings with C-level executives that Diane wasn't invited to, and as the sting of Diane's rejection waned, I realized that my patience, long-suffering, and faith grew in its wake. Not only that, as my character strengthened and my speaking ministry flourished, I learned that releasing me into speaking was only *part* of God's plan.

After a year of faithfully serving Diane—the person who had hurt me so deeply—she was demoted as team leader and moved to a different part of the company as an individual contributor. Her boss came and told me the team was going to be restructured under a newly created leadership role. And then she asked me if I would be willing to serve in that role. Not only did God use Diane's rejection to position me in the public sphere, but he *also* used her rejection to position me for a higher level of leadership in the professional sphere.

Diane's rejection set off a cascade of destiny in my life. Your rejection is positioning you too. The door that someone shut, the person who walked away, the invitation you didn't receive—it all serves a purpose. Instead of holding a grudge, discipline yourself to ask God, "Lord, what are you positioning me for?" Let's OPEN this gift, together.

OPEN THE GIFT

Take a moment to identify a past or present rejection experience to which you can apply the OPEN framework to help you discover how it positions you for purpose.

Observe

Take a moment to observe your thoughts about the role your rejection experience has played in positioning you for purpose.

1. What lie have you believed about why this rejection happened? Considering what you read in this chapter,

what *truth can you use to combat* the lie you've been believing?

2. What one mental talk track have you been rehearsing that has allowed your rejection to limit your beliefs about what is possible for you?

3. What story have you told yourself to explain how your life would have been better if the rejection had not happened?

4. After considering how God uses rejection to position you for purpose, how could your life have been worse if the rejection had not happened?

Pray

We often don't notice God working on our behalf because we are so fixated on our pain that it becomes a distraction. But Jeremiah 29:11 says, "'For I know the plans I have for you,' declares the Lord, 'plans to prosper you and not to harm you, plans to give you hope and a future.'"

Take a moment to go before God with what you have observed, and pray for him to help you see how he has been using rejection to position you for purpose. As a guide for your prayer time, you can offer the following prayer:

Lord, help me see how the rejection I've been pained to remember has been serving your purpose for my life. Help me remember the ways you have used what others meant for evil—to harm me—as an occasion to grow me and unleash my destiny. I am grateful for your sovereignty and that you know what is best for me, even when it feels like it's the worst thing that could have happened. You are good, and your mercy endures forever.

Although rejection can leave you feeling like you missed your *one* chance, the Bible tells us that God orders our steps (Psalm 37:23–24). Remember this: when rejection leaves you feeling overlooked or hidden, God knows exactly where you are.

Explore

Dig a bit deeper to explore how your rejection experience has given you the gift of positioning you for purpose:

1. How has this rejection experience strengthened your character or enabled you to build a new skill or ability you did not have before?
2. What insight has this rejection experience given you about yourself?
3. How has God revealed his goodness in the midst of this rejection?
4. What new opportunities are available to you because of what this rejection has taught you?
5. What old opportunities did you turn down that this rejection has caused you to reconsider?

Name

The insights you have gained through observing your thoughts, praying for God's wisdom, and exploring the lessons from your rejection have produced a rich treasure of lessons from which to pull. Now name your next step. What one action step can you take over the next two weeks to partner with God in making your pain purposeful?

Maybe you now realize that being repeatedly turned down for an internal job transfer is God positioning you for employment elsewhere. Update your résumé this week, and send it to prospective employers this weekend.

Maybe you now realize that your boyfriend's refusal to be accountable for his hurtful actions is God positioning you for a new relationship. Find a new place to live, and pack your belongings to move out next week.

Maybe you now realize that not being invited to your dad's home for holiday gatherings is God positioning you to serve the homeless at the local soup kitchen on those days. Contact the organization today, and commit to serving food on the holidays for the rest of the year.

As you thoughtfully consider how rejection is positioning you for purpose, let's OPEN the second gift: revealing people's role in your destiny.

CHAPTER

GIFT #2

Revealing People's Role in Your Destiny

I had just finished speaking at a major women's conference in San Francisco, California, when a woman in ministry whom I had admired from afar for years approached me with a wide smile. "You did a wonderful job," she said. "Let's keep in touch. Here's my number. Call me anytime."

When she turned around to walk away, heart bubbles of joy flooded my body. Had it not been for the laws of physics, I'm pretty sure I would have lifted into the air out of excitement. *Finally*, someone had taken an interest in me. *Finally*, someone had offered to take me under their wing. It was an answer to my prayers.

Over the next few months, I made a point to text her to see how I could pray for her, and one day she asked me to pray for a lump she had found in her breast. I prayed in earnest and checked on her every few days until I found out she was having surgery to remove cancerous tumors in her breasts. After the surgery, I had flowers delivered to her hospital room, and after she was discharged, I had flowers delivered to her home.

Two weeks after discharge, I ended up in her city for a speaking engagement, so I texted her to ask if she felt up to having me stop by and visit. She responded immediately and enthusiastically and gave me her address. I stopped by a boutique on the way to her home and bought a piece of jewelry as a gift for her. During my three-hour visit, we talked about life, family, ministry, and more. I left convinced I had found a new friend and mentor.

As the months went by, the release date approached for my first book, *Success from the Inside Out*. That meant it was also nearing the time for my *least favorite* part of the book release process: soliciting book endorsements. This part of the process involves seeking a one- to two-sentence statement of support from a dozen or so prominent people for featuring in the book and book promotions. I don't like soliciting endorsements because the very thought of someone saying no heightens my rejection anxiety. Although it happens rarely, when a no does happen, it feels like a personal rejection because while an endorsement affirms the importance of the book's *message*, it affirms the credibility of the *author* even more.

Despite my initial anxiety, I was certain I could count on the endorsement of my friend and mentor. I texted her one morning and said, "Hi! I'm really excited to share that my forthcoming book is heading to press soon. I would be super honored if you would be willing to consider offering a one- to two-sentence endorsement of the message. It will be due a month from now."

About two hours later, she said, "Congratulations, Nona! That is wonderful news. I'm working on my own book right now and don't think I'll be able to find time to write an endorsement for you."

I read and reread her text through a mild state of bewilderment. Although I responded with an understanding text message, the experience left me questioning why she didn't feel I was worth the time. By turning down my request to endorse my book, she was actually turning down endorsing *me*. I shrugged off how I was feeling as a misunderstanding on my part and decided not to dwell on it. Having gone through the process of writing a book, I understood how time-consuming it can be. But I was still hurt.

A few weeks later, a mutual friend of ours shared a photo of herself with my mentor on Instagram and thanked her for endorsing her forthcoming book. Shortly after, my mentor did an Instagram Live with another mutual friend to help promote the friend's book. Over the coming months I saw several more people share graphics of my mentor's two-sentence endorsements of their books. I shrugged it off again, telling myself that they must have known her longer than I had. But it still hurt.

I began to wonder what all those people had that I didn't. When I investigated, I noticed the common thread: they all had exponentially larger social followings than I had.

I had initially been *so* excited to have her give me her phone number. I thought the many conversations we'd had up until that point meant she was someone I could count on. But after realizing my ask didn't rise to the top of her "yes" pile because I didn't have enough notoriety, I felt like I had been left out in the field by myself while everyone else was invited to her party.

I have found that rejection hurts most when we believe we need the person who rejected us. Since *Success from the Inside Out* was my first book, I felt like my friend's endorsement would be crucial for establishing credibility for me and my message. But, in this experience, I learned an important lesson. *When the person you think you need walks away, you discover the only One who matters.*

> When the person you think you need walks away, you discover the only One who matters.

GOD'S VIP LIST

Have you ever been to a professional sports tournament? Having been to several, I can safely say that the experience is different depending on who you are and the type of ticket you hold.

I once took my oldest son to see his favorite basketball player, Giannis Antetokounmpo, play against the Orlando Magic. We had general admission tickets and stood outside in a long line for quite some time waiting to go through security. When we finally made it inside the arena, we bought two bags of popcorn and two bottles of water for about $230 (*slight exaggeration*), then made our way to the middle stands to settle into our hard seats. Other patrons had to step over us to get to their seats, so we were regularly faced with strangers' backsides or bellies as they scooted down the row.

It was a very different world when my husband and I were invited to sit courtside at an Oklahoma City Thunder game.

First, we were offered special VIP parking in a garage right next to the arena. Then instead of waiting in line, we walked up to a special VIP entrance where our things were quickly passed through an X-ray machine. After the twenty seconds that took, security escorted us to a private lounge where a James Beard Award–winning chef had prepared the meal for the evening. Drinks of all types were free and plentiful, and when it was time for the game, security escorted us to our plush seats. When the game ended, we were escorted to a private exit, where we climbed into our car and left without fighting traffic.

When I was on the Oklahoma City Thunder's VIP list, I experienced a number of amazing perks because of the price that was paid for my ticket. But as amazing as those perks were, they don't begin to compare to the perks of being on *God's* VIP list. Unlike any VIP list created by a human being, God's VIP list is not based on wealth or celebrity. It is simply based on the condition of your heart.

After the prophet Samuel asked Jesse to have his sons pass before him, the first son he saw was the eldest, Eliab. When Samuel looked at Eliab's outward appearance, he was convinced that Eliab was God's next chosen king of Israel (1 Samuel 16:6). He was undoubtedly attractive and probably even had some of the features that made King Saul stand out (1 Samuel 9:2). He *looked* royal, but he was far from it. God told Samuel in 1 Samuel 16:7, "Do not consider his appearance or his height, for I have rejected him. The Lord does not look at the things people look at. People look at the outward appearance, but the Lord looks at the heart."

Even though Eliab was pleasing to Samuel's eye and his

name was on Samuel's VIP list, it was *David* who was pleasing to God's heart and had his name on God's VIP list. God chose David because he was the fulfillment of 1 Samuel 13:14: he was a man after God's own heart. God didn't choose David because man had chosen him. *God chose David to prove that God's opinion is the only one that matters.*

God chose David to prove that God's opinion is the only one that matters.

After Samuel had met seven of Jesse's sons, the Bible says in 1 Samuel 16:10–11,

> "The LORD has not chosen these." So [Samuel] asked Jesse, "Are these all the sons you have?"
>
> "There is still the youngest," Jesse answered. "He is tending the sheep."
>
> Samuel said, "Send for him; we will not sit down until he arrives."

I imagine this moment was pregnant with frustration as Jesse and his sons were forced to stand and wait for someone they had not even invited to the sacrifice.

> So he sent for him and had him brought in. He was glowing with health and had a fine appearance and handsome features.
>
> Then the LORD said, "Rise and anoint him; this is the one." (1 Samuel 16:12)

Samuel was impressed by David's physical appearance, but it wasn't his physical appearance that qualified him in the eyes of God. God saw what Samuel couldn't see.

So Samuel took the horn of oil and anointed him in the
presence of his brothers, and from that day on the Spirit of
the LORD came powerfully upon David. (1 Samuel 16:13)

Pay close attention to something. The Bible says Samuel
anointed David *in the presence of* his brothers. Samuel anointed
David in the presence of the people who had left him out in a
field tending sheep by himself while their father invited them
to have an audience with God's prophet. Everything God
does is purposeful, and when I consider this scene, I believe
the reason why God had Samuel anoint David in the presence
of the people who had rejected him was because God wanted
to teach David and his family an important truth.

No matter who overlooks you, abandons you, or leaves
you in a field by yourself tending sheep, when God is for you,
no one can oppose you. When God is for
you, the people who rejected you will have
to watch him promote you. When God is
for you, *the favor of God will make your
enemies your audience.*

**The favor of God will
make your enemies
your audience.**

> The manager who denied your promotion, only to have
> their boss promote you anyway because of your
> impressive record of impact.
> The guy who broke up with you over text and now has
> to watch you walk down the aisle with his college
> friend who asked you to marry him.
> The teacher who told you that you would never be
> anything but then showed up to your book signing
> and asked you to sign their copy.

That last one happened to me. I couldn't help but thank God that he has the final say in my life. And he has the final say in *your* life too!

Many people love to quote Psalm 23 to remind themselves that God is faithful in trials and tribulations. Pay special attention to verse 5, which says, "You prepare a table before me in the presence of my enemies." When you learn to see rejection as a gift, you will realize that the people who rejected you are simply the audience for whom God is preparing the table of your purpose. Instead of lamenting who rejected you, praise God for what he is preparing because of them!

> **What God created you to do is not dependent on the acceptance of other people.**

What God created you to do is not dependent on the acceptance of other people. While people can reject *you*, no one can reject *your purpose*. Your purpose is never hindered by someone who walks away from you. Your purpose is never hindered by a situation that didn't work out for you. Instead of blocking your future, the gift of rejection simply reveals the end of some people's roles in your destiny.

AN (UNEXPECTED) ANSWER TO PRAYER

When my husband retired from his corporate leadership role to become a full-time pastor in October 2015, our family lost half his salary. Thankfully, God promoted me into a role that more than made up for what we lost. Although most weeks I had to travel to Washington, DC, New York, and Atlanta for meetings, I was a constant fixture at our church.

I led our women's ministry, led the praise and worship ministry, and designed all our marketing materials. This meant my weekday evenings were filled with meetings and rehearsals. On the weekends, I had primary responsibility for our young children so my husband could officiate the many weddings and funerals at our church. I offered a loving hug as people entered and exited the building every Sunday. Between work and church, I had no days off. I was exhausted and prayed for God to send someone who could take on the praise and worship ministry so I could breathe a little.

One Sunday a new family visited. I noticed them before service and made my way over to offer a welcome and hug. They returned for several weeks and, one day, told my husband and me that they wanted to join the church. I remember thinking something was sad about the wife, Janice. I am a very empathic person, so even though she was polite, I sensed an emotional wall within her. As I got to know her, she validated what I had sensed. "I've built countless praise teams and choirs for churches, but every time things started going well, the pastor would remove me without explanation," she shared, visibly bothered by the memories. "I got to the point that I felt so hurt, I decided I would never join a church again. But then my husband found out about your church, and I decided to visit with him. You were so nice and genuine the first time we visited. I had never experienced that from a First Lady before. I felt like this was home."

Given her painful church experiences, I took a deep interest in her and wanted to be an instrument God could use to help her heal from past pain. I began taking her out to lunch and spending time with her just to listen to her story. After a couple of months, she showed up to the praise team rehearsal I was leading and sat in the audience while we practiced. My music director recognized her and told me I needed to invite her up to sing. She initially said no, but within fifteen minutes, she had a mic in her hand. When she started to sing, everyone's jaws dropped. Janice couldn't just sing. Janice could *sang*—the term we use in Black culture when someone's voice leaves you speechless.

After a few Sundays of her singing with us, I asked her to consider serving as praise team leader, and I was overjoyed when she agreed to help me lead the team. Several members of her family also joined the team, and before long our sound was next level. They were all incredible singers. Not only that, but her husband was a musician. He started to play for the team, and between her voice and his playing, I was in heaven. Janice always sat next to me in church. We became so close with her family that we spent most Sunday afternoons at our home or theirs. For the first time I could see relief in sight for the many leadership roles I held at the church. She was an answer to my prayers! Or so I thought.

Four months after Janice agreed to serve as the praise team leader, my life radically changed when I was offered the newly created role of head of global faith partnerships at Facebook. At least once per month I spent my workweek in California, then took an early flight on Thursday mornings to get back to Florida in time to race to church for praise team rehearsal at 7:00 p.m. Some weeks, international travel didn't allow me to return for rehearsal at all. As my ministry-speaking schedule increased, I missed a few Sundays, but I would always call Janice to let her know whenever I couldn't make it. I slowly started noticing a negative shift in her attitude toward me.

There were times when she became visibly irritated when she saw me at church or rehearsal. She even voiced disappointment that my career was more of a priority than the praise team. Although my career was supporting my family, that didn't matter to her.

"I'm leaving the church," she told my husband over a call one day.

"Leaving? Why?" he asked, caught off guard.

"I just can't stay at a church where the First Lady is so . . . not involved," she responded.

"What do you mean by that?" he probed.

"She was supposed to lead worship a few Sundays but had to back out because she was traveling somewhere. It just seems like she has other priorities. That doesn't work for me."

My husband texted me the news: "Janice says she's leaving because . . . you have a job."

As I read the text, my plane started taxiing to the runway in Chicago, so I responded to my husband with the only thing I could muster: "Okay." I turned my phone on airplane mode and sighed.

Janice's role as worship leader made her highly visible in our church, so her choice to leave was devastating. Her departure not only caused a major disruption to our praise team, it also caused a major disruption for me too. I had to quickly figure out how to step back in and lead the team in the midst of a grueling travel schedule. On top of that, I was deeply hurt that she blamed *me* for her decision. Instead of discussing her issues with me, she just hit the eject button.

No call.

No text.

No smoke signal.

No goodbye.

It took months of prayer and self-work to get to a healthy emotional state where I was no longer angry or hurt by her leaving. It also took a lot of time to stop blaming myself for her choice. But that change happened only after I started to OPEN the gift of her rejection and allowed it to teach me. *A person's decision to leave you is the end of their role in your life.*

> **A person's decision to leave you is the end of their role in your life.**

ATTACHED VERSUS ASSIGNED

Have you ever tried to keep someone in your life, only to have them disappear when you needed them?

Maybe you sacrificed the sleep you desperately needed to attend a friend's last-minute birthday party in hopes of making them happy, but a few months later that same "friend" couldn't attend *your* birthday dinner.

Maybe you let your coworker have the $200 they needed to make their rent payment, but after you gave them the money, they didn't seem capable of responding to your texts.

Maybe you felt your boyfriend growing distant, so you cooked him dinner and ended the night with sex despite him not taking you out in weeks or ever introducing you to his family.

I believe there are two types of people in our lives when it comes to relationships: those who are *attached* and those who are *assigned*. When a person is *attached* to you, they are in the relationship for the benefits it gives *them*. Attached people are along for the ride, but the moment your ride isn't taking them where they want to go, they detach. Their attachment was never about you, it was about the value you brought to them.

The "friend" whose birthday party you attended enjoyed the gift you bought them, but they didn't attend your birthday because they didn't see how spending money on you could benefit them.

The coworker whose rent you paid enjoyed staying in their apartment, but they didn't return your texts because they didn't see how communication with you benefited them.

The man you fed and pleased sexually enjoyed having you take care of him, but he didn't take you out because he didn't see how spending money on you benefited him.

In each of these cases, their attachment was about how their connection to you benefited *them*. Because of this, their *detachment* from you was about them too. When Janice detached from me, it was because she no longer had the benefit of access to me.

People detach from you when the relationship no longer serves their goals.

People detach from you when the relationship no longer serves their goals.

On the flip side, when a person is *assigned* to you, they aren't in the relationship for what they can get *out* of you;

they are in the relationship for what they can *contribute* to you. When a person is assigned to you, God has placed them in your life and given them a desire to support and encourage you. Not because of what you *do* for them but because of *who you are* to them.

> The friend who gathers your loved ones and throws a surprise birthday party to celebrate you.
>
> The coworker who tells your boss how amazing you are without letting you know they're going to do it.
>
> The man who finds out you're sick and has flowers and chicken soup delivered to you while he's out of state for work.

Your friend does not throw the party so that you will do it for them. Your coworker does not give you kudos so that you will do it for them. That man does not take care of you so that you will do it for him.

Unlike attached people, assigned people don't hit the eject button just because things get hard. Their assignment to you is revealed by a care that is not quid pro quo.

One of the worst mistakes we often make is allowing an attached person's detaching from us to trigger our insecurity. When this happens, we succumb to the desperation to be accepted and shift our energy *away* from the assigned people in our lives to channel more energy in the direction of the detaching people.

A case in point: when I felt Janice starting to detach, I started calling and texting her more. When I was in town, I made sure to find time for her. I greeted her extra warmly when I saw her at church. I stopped calling and texting other friends as much so I could try to patch things up with Janice. I would turn down their asks to get together for lunch so I could spend time with Janice. But, even after I did all of that, she *still* left.

When you OPEN the gift of rejection, you will find that you can sacrifice everything you love for attached people, and they will *still* walk away from you. Once you come to terms with this truth, you can accept their decision as their choice, *not* your fault.

When I OPENed the gift of Janice's rejection, I had to ask myself why I had worked so hard to win the approval of someone who had a track record for discarding pastors and their wives. I had to come to terms with my own belief that being chosen by her made me somehow worthy. That was a lie.

God is bigger than the friendship of someone who doesn't want to give it.

> God is bigger than the friendship of someone who doesn't want to give it.

Just like a basketball team has only so many players on their roster, you will have only so many assigned people on the roster of your life. Instead of holding a spot for someone who is attached only for the benefits you can give them, accept the gift of their rejection as an opportunity for God to fill that roster spot with someone new.

No matter who walked away, overlooked you, or didn't invite you, you are on God's VIP list. God loves you so much that the Bible says Christ died for you while you were *still* a sinner (Romans 5:8). What does this mean?

Christ died for us when *we* walked away from *him*.

Christ died for us when *we* overlooked *him*.

Christ died for us when *we* didn't invite *him* into our lives.

When others turn their back on you, you can OPEN the gift of their rejection and allow it to lead you back to the One who never left.

OPEN THE GIFT

Take a moment to identify a past or present rejection experience to which you can apply the OPEN framework to help you discover how it reveals people's role in your destiny.

Observe

Take a moment to observe your thoughts about the role your rejection experience has played in revealing people's role in your destiny:

1. What lie have you believed about the role that person was supposed to play in your life? Considering what you read in this chapter, what *truth can you use to combat* the lie you've been believing?
2. What one mental talk track have you been rehearsing that makes you believe you need them in your life?
3. What story have you told yourself to explain how having them in your life would have made your life better?
4. After considering how God uses rejection to reveal people's role in your destiny, how could your life have been worse if they had stayed in it?
5. What role (if any) did you play in the demise of the relationship?

Pray

When people walk away from us, it can feel like the future we imagined with them is in jeopardy. But 1 Corinthians 2:9 says, "'What no eye has seen, what no ear has heard, and what no human mind has conceived'—the things God has prepared for those who love him." In other words, it is not a *person* who holds our future. It is *God*.

Take a moment to go before God with what you have observed, and pray for him to help you clearly see how he has been using rejection to reveal people's role in your destiny. As a guide for your prayer time, you can offer the following prayer:

> *Lord, help me discern between attachments and assignments. Help me release those who have detached and embrace those who are assigned. Heal me from the pain of abandonment, because those who attached were only completing their role in my life. Give me the grace to leave the past where it lives and walk toward the future you have for me, a future filled with hope and purpose.*

When we focus on the people who walked away, we can lose sight of the people who have never left. Ask God to reveal the people who are assigned to you so you can invest your attention and energy into nurturing those relationships.

Explore

Dig a bit deeper to explore how your rejection experience has given you the gift of revealing people's role in your destiny with the following questions:

1. Is there something you were relying on that person to do for you? What have you discovered you have the ability to do for yourself now that they have detached?
2. What insight has this rejection experience given you about yourself, and how can you show up better for the people assigned to you?
3. Who is investing more time, energy, and effort into building a relationship with you than you are with them?
4. Which relationships might you need to let go of because those people are receiving benefits they aren't returning to you?
5. How has God revealed his goodness in the midst of this rejection?

Name

The insights you have gained through observing your thoughts, praying for God's wisdom, and exploring the lessons from your rejection have produced a rich treasure of lessons from which to pull. Now name your next step. What one action step can you take over the next two weeks to partner with God in making your pain purposeful?

Maybe you now realize that a person you counted as a friend shows up only when they need something from you. Sit down with them this week to discuss their behavior and explain your expectations for the relationship going forward (should you decide to remain friends).

Maybe you now realize that *you* haven't been a good friend to someone who has been consistently there for you. Invite them to dinner this weekend to thank them for their friendship and learn more about how you can better serve them.

Maybe you now realize you have been hanging on to a romantic relationship where only the other person is benefiting. Take time over the next week to explore what you believe about yourself that has caused you to settle, then commit to not settling anymore.

As you thoughtfully consider how rejection is revealing people's roles in your destiny, let's OPEN the third gift: anchoring your identity.

CHAPTER

GIFT #3

Anchoring Your Identity

"I can't do this anymore. I'm done."

I was in my third year of college and thought I'd met the man I would marry. When I first saw him, he was sitting on a bench on Turlington Plaza, a popular gathering spot on the University of Florida's campus. He was talking and laughing with his fraternity brothers. His bright purple-and-gold shirt caught my attention, but I didn't think he noticed me as I hurried by on my way to organic chemistry.

"Excuse me," he said as he stood up and walked in my direction.

"Yes?" I asked.

"What's your name?"

"Nona."

"You're the best thing I've seen out here all day, Nona," he said, flashing a set of perfect white teeth. "My name is Michael."

I felt myself blush. "Thank you," I said. "Nice to meet you, Michael."

"You already ate lunch?" he asked.

"Yes. I'm heading to class."

"Oh, okay. Well, I'd love to talk if you have some time. Maybe tomorrow? Meet here and get some lunch?"

"Uhhh . . . I have class around lunch time. I'm not finished until three p.m."

"Cool, three it is. Where will you be? I'll come meet you there," he said. "Can I get your number?"

Although I didn't make it a habit to give my number to random guys, something about Michael felt safe. I gave him my number and smiled as I waved goodbye.

He met me after class the next day, and we grabbed a late lunch at the nearby cafeteria. We talked and laughed for more than three hours before I told him I needed to get back to my dorm to study for an exam I had the next day. He walked me back as the streetlights came on.

When we reached the lobby he said, "I really enjoyed getting to know you tonight, Nona. I'm looking forward to getting to know you more."

Before I reached my dorm room door, he texted me to ask to meet again the following day. I smiled as my heart filled with excitement. For the next few weeks, he was consistently affectionate, attentive, and kind. I woke every morning to a message on my phone: "Good morning, beautiful."

But one day he didn't show up at our lunch date as planned. I waited for thirty minutes, watching the entrance and my phone between bites of my chicken sandwich. When I could no longer wait, I grabbed my things and left the cafeteria to head to class. I called him on my way there.

"Hey, Nona," he said on the first ring.

"Hey . . . just checking on you. What happened?"

"With what?"

"Lunch today. You didn't show up."

"Oh! I got tied up . . . helping my . . . frat brother with a project."

"Okay, well, can you call or text me next time? I would have stayed at my dorm and studied."

"I mean . . . I didn't do it intentionally. Why are you so upset?"

"I'm not upset. Things happen. I'm just asking if you can let me know if something comes up next time so I can better plan my day."

"I mean . . . sorry for unintentionally not calling you. I didn't do it on purpose. You just need to chill."

My heart raced in my chest as his words settled in my mind. Instead of simply apologizing for his lack of consideration and the inconvenience it had created for me, he decided the real problem was that *I* needed to chill.

"Michael, I had other things I could have been doing. All I'm saying is I would appreciate you—"

The sound of silence filled my ears. He had hung up on me.

I walked to my class in stunned silence as a pulsation in my head grew to a throbbing pain. After class ended and I walked back to my dorm, I sat on my bed in confusion, trying to understand where I had gone wrong in the conversation with Michael.

Was my tone angry? Did I say the wrong things? What did I do to make him hang up on me?

The confusion of rejection can make you think you deserved it.

> **The confusion of rejection can make you think you deserved it.**

I pulled out my biology textbook and tried to study, but my mind kept getting dragged back to him hanging up on me. I pulled out my phone and texted him: "Michael, I don't know what happened earlier, but I was just saying I wish you could have told me something came up. I'm sorry if I came across as angry. I wasn't. I was just trying to ask you to let me know next time. That's all. I'm sorry."

I checked my texts every few minutes, but there was no reply. Sleep eluded me that night.

As I was getting ready for class the next morning, my phone dinged with a text from Michael. "Good morning, beautiful. Listen, I know you didn't mean to come at me like you did yesterday. Let's meet for lunch today. I'll see you at one."

Something within me felt both relieved and confused. I was relieved that he wasn't angry with me anymore, but I was confused by the fact that he felt the issue was how I came at him, not with how he stood me up. When I walked into the cafeteria, he was nowhere to be found, so I grabbed a turkey sandwich, waited fifteen minutes, then started eating. Ten minutes later, he strolled in and walked up to my table with a smile. "Hey, baby. You look great. Wait . . . you already ate? Without me?"

"Well, I waited for about fifteen minutes, then I wasn't sure if something came up again, so I went ahead and ate."

"Wow. So you didn't even care that I was waiting to eat with you? That I was hungry too? You just went ahead and ate?"

"Well . . . no . . . I was here at one like you said. I waited fiftee—"

"You know, Nona, this isn't how I do things. If you were late, I would wait for you."

"Michael, I didn't know what time you were—"

"Just forget it," he said as he walked away and stormed out the front door.

I lost whatever appetite I had left and threw the rest of my food in the trash. My mind was reeling and my heart was pounding as I pulled out my phone to call him. After one ring, it went to voicemail. I texted him and said, "Michael, I'm sorry. I didn't know if you were coming. I just . . . I don't know what's going on."

Tears filled the corners of my eyes as I made my way to class. I couldn't focus on what the teacher was saying because my mind was drowning in confusion and disbelief. I wondered how someone who had initially been so sweet and consistent could suddenly become so cruel and erratic. What had I done to make him so angry, and most importantly, how could I change it?

He didn't contact me for the rest of the day, so before I went to sleep, I texted him and asked, "Before I assume anything, are you not contacting me on purpose or just because you got busy today?"

Twenty minutes later, he responded with, "Both. I don't have the energy to fight with you. I have a lot on my plate right now, and you're not in a good place for me mentally/emotionally."

I tossed and turned that night, replaying the days of rejection I had experienced. I couldn't make sense of what I had done wrong to set him off so many times. To make matters worse, friends told me about seeing him around campus hugged up on other girls. It was too much for me. I figured that the only way to make the relationship work was to try to bend myself in whatever direction Michael was leaning at the moment. I committed myself to being a better girlfriend by anticipating his needs and doing everything I could not to upset him.

Though I had been the type of person to rarely check my phone throughout the day, I started watching it like a hawk in case he called or texted so I could immediately respond. If I didn't immediately answer his call or text, he would text me with, "Oh, so I guess we broke up now???" My 4.0 GPA started to slip because if he told me to meet him somewhere, I would leave class early to get there on time. In the super rare instance that he arrived before me, he immediately texted, "Where are you?" and would remind me that making him wait was disrespectful.

I found myself contorting my time, personality, and conversations to fit around his ever-changing, unclear expectations of me. He created a vicious cycle of drawing me in, only to push me away. I became so emotionally dysregulated that I stopped bringing up anything he did that I felt was wrong, out of fear he would reject me again. I tried to be upbeat and agreeable with him whenever he lashed out at me for one thing or another, but he still treated me like an opponent in a fight I didn't know I was in.

Despite knowing how important communication was to

me, he started punishing me by letting days go by without contacting me, only to pop up with a text asking, "Did you miss me?" or "Are you done being silly now?"

Sometimes people reject you to control you.

After months of losing myself within his definition of a good girlfriend, my

Sometimes people reject you to control you.

grades became so bad that I had to withdraw from summer classes so my GPA wouldn't tank. I was constantly anxious as he entered and exited my life without rhyme or reason. Although I was actively involved in my church before meeting Michael, I had slowly stopped attending and serving so I could spend more time with him on the weekends.

One morning, after three days of silent punishment from Michael for the infraction of not acting happy enough at dinner, I sat in my dorm by myself and realized I was utterly isolated. I no longer had a church family or close friends. Although school had been a source of excitement for me and I loved learning, I had withdrawn from classes and spent most of my time in my dorm room just waiting for Michael to contact me.

Tears rolled down my cheeks as I reflected on how often he had blamed me for having a bad attitude when I was sad, instead of asking why I was sad or trying to cheer me up. I was sad because of *him*. No matter what I did or said, he would always cast me as the guilty party despite him yelling at me, talking over me, and cutting me off if I dared to try to express myself.

As I sat on my bed in the quiet of my room, reflexively checking my phone every two minutes for his nonexistent text, something stirred within me. Although I had walked away from my church home, I still knew the voice of God. I heard quietly but firmly in my heart "This isn't my perfect will for you." Those words echoed in my mind, then reverberated down to my fingers until I picked up my phone, opened my texts, and found the thread with Michael that was full of my apologies but devoid of his response.

In that moment, alone with nothing but my pain and God, I realized that all of Michael's mind games had caused me to shrink myself down to fit inside the too-small box of his low opinion of me. Although my flesh was weak and wanted Michael, my spirit was willing and wanted God. And I was no longer willing to participate in a fight of Michael's making. I mustered the shred of energy I had left as my fingers glided across the keyboard: "I can't do this anymore. I'm done."

Block. Delete.

THE REJECTION GAME

Have you ever experienced a relationship where the only time you received love and validation was when you did what the other person wanted, where you had to mold yourself to their ideal image of you to get their attention?

Maybe you worked hard in school to make your dad proud, but instead of celebrating your six As, he wanted to know why you made one B. Even though you worked extremely hard for your grades, his disapproval created the sense that nothing less than perfection was worthy of his attention, causing you to believe that you're a failure unless you're the first or the best.

Maybe you graduated college with an architecture degree, but instead of celebrating your accomplishment, your grandmother didn't attend the graduation because she said being an architect wasn't respectable like being a physician. Even though you love architecture and graduated at the top of your class, her disapproval made you question your decision and feel ashamed of your degree.

Maybe you gave birth to twins, but instead of celebrating the miracle of your children's birth, your husband expressed disappointment with the stretch marks on your belly. Even though you worked hard to get back into shape after giving birth, his disapproval made you self-conscious of your body, causing you to put away the two-piece bathing suits you loved.

People's rejection of parts of us that make us who we are feels personal because it *is* personal; they are rejecting the very attributes that comprise our identity. In response to their rejection, we tend to internalize their assessment as evidence of our unworthiness. This can lead us to modulate our personalities, interests, accomplishments, and desires down to the level of their opinion to try to please them. But the sad, sinister side of some human relationships is found in an unfortunate truth. *Even if you do everything someone tells you to do, they can still walk away from you.*

Even if you do everything someone tells you to do, they can still walk away from you.

For some people, rejection is like a game where the object is to win by controlling you. The term *narcissist* has entered popular vernacular in recent years, but it is typically applied inappropriately. Many people think narcissism is simply when a person is being egotistical or arrogant, but narcissism goes much deeper and causes an incredible amount of harm to the victim. You see, unlike psychological disorders like depression or schizophrenia, instead of affecting the person who *has* the disorder, narcissism affects the *other people* in the narcissist's life.

As described by *Psychology Today*, "Narcissism is characterized by a grandiose sense of self-importance, a lack of empathy for others, a need for excessive admiration, and the belief that one is unique and deserving of special treatment."[1] What makes narcissism so insidious is that narcissists force other people to shape their lives around the narcissist's beliefs about themselves. In other words, a narcissist uses the people in their lives to build monuments of grandeur unto themselves. Because of this, when a person doesn't make the narcissist look as good as they believe they are, disapproval is swift, visceral, and destructive. How does it show itself?

In the case of your B in school, your father wasn't disappointed because of what that grade meant for *your* GPA; he was disappointed that he couldn't say *he* was the father of a straight A student. He wasn't able to use your report card as a monument of grandeur unto himself.

In the case of your architecture degree, your grandmother wasn't disappointed because she believed it would limit *your* career options; she was disappointed that *she* wouldn't be able to tell her friends that you are a physician like their grandchildren. She wasn't able to use your degree as a monument of grandeur unto herself.

In the case of your stretch marks, your husband wasn't disappointed because of how they made *you* look; he was disappointed because *his* trophy wife had a perceived flaw.

He wasn't able to use your perfect body as a monument of grandeur unto himself.

Awareness of the motives behind their behavior matters because if you don't understand this, you will assume that their disapproval of you is because something is wrong with you. You will try to pinpoint the parts of your identity that need to change in order for them to approve of you, when the truth is that *their disapproval has nothing to do with you at all*. Their disapproval is the result of their distorted sense of entitlement to the admiration they can receive through you.

When you are dealing with a person who simply views you as a means to an end—their own self-aggrandizement—you can check all their boxes and *still* get rejected. If you secure your identity to another person's approval or opinion of you, you will find yourself battling insecurity, because people's approval often changes like the currents of the ocean. Why? *People often approve of others based on self-interest.*

People often approve of others based on self-interest.

When I first met Michael, I was president of my sorority and a well-known student leader on campus. I regularly spoke at campus events and held prestigious leadership positions with a number of influential organizations. Although I didn't know who he was, Michael knew *exactly* who I was. Within the first week of getting to know each other, he told me that he had been watching me for a while, waiting for an opportunity to introduce himself. He even remarked how cute of a couple we made because he was president of his fraternity. He was with me because *I made him look good.*

As our relationship progressed, I noticed that he often made our communication about himself—asking if I missed him, asking me how he looked, telling me about the awards and recognitions he received. He asked very little about me and, instead, told me about myself, specifically about whatever flaws he perceived I had.

"Nona, you should listen more. You talk too much." This was said after he talked for twenty-eight minutes of a thirty-two-minute conversation that he ended in frustration because I reminded him I had listened most of the time.

"Nona, you complain too much. You always have a problem." This was said when I told him what was bothering me about my day after he had asked me how my day was.

"Nona, you are too needy. I'm giving you as much time as I have." This was after I asked him to find more time than the one- to two-minute conversations we would have every other day near the end of our relationship.

Since I didn't know any better and believed his assessment that I was the problem, I took his feedback to heart and only spoke concisely when he asked me a direct question.

In the rare event that he asked me about my day, I learned to say, "It was good," no matter how bad it was.

Instead of asking for more time, I made sure I immediately answered when he called so I could get whatever crumbs of time he offered me.

Rejection will make you lose yourself *out of fear of losing someone else.*

> Rejection will make you lose *yourself* out of fear of losing someone else.

By the time I came to my senses in that dorm room on that summer morning, I realized there was nothing I could do or say to make Michael believe differently about me. So I decided to do the one thing I had forgotten to do the entire time; I decided to be who *God* called me to be. I wasn't the overbearing, negative, or needy person Michael said I was. I was chosen by God, part of a royal priesthood (1 Peter 2:9). I decided I would wrap my heart around the truth that what Michael thought about me didn't change what God said about me.

The manipulation and control tactics Michael used were meant to break me down so he could remake me in an image of his own design, but instead, his rejection served to anchor me in the truth of God's perfect design of me.

WHO DO YOU THINK YOU ARE?

Let's get honest for a moment. Can you think back to a situation where you lost yourself in an effort to gain the acceptance of someone else?

Maybe you wanted to be accepted by a coworker so badly that you started drinking with them even though you don't like alcohol.

Maybe you wanted to be accepted by classmates so badly that you started using foul language to seem "cool."

Maybe you wanted to be accepted by your cousin so badly that you joined her in gossiping about other family members to get into her good graces.

We change who we are in the hope of fitting neatly enough within their opinions that they will approve of us. But when that coworker stops inviting you out and those classmates start calling you names and that cousin starts talking about *you* behind *your* back, there is a gift in their rejection. What if, instead of changing yourself to try to win them over, you allowed their rejection to free you to be exactly who you are?

Like David. In 1 Samuel 17:17, David's father Jesse told him to take lunch to his brothers who were fighting in Israel's army. David left for the battlefield early in the morning after leaving the flock of sheep he had been caring for with another shepherd. When he arrived, he ran out to the battle line to see what was happening and started talking to his brothers.

> As he was talking with them, Goliath, the Philistine champion from Gath, stepped out from his lines and shouted his usual defiance, and David heard it. Whenever the Israelites saw the man, they all fled from him in great fear. (1 Samuel 17:23–24)

David got his first look at Goliath when he allowed his curiosity to take him to the battle line.

> Now the Israelites had been saying, "Do you see how this man keeps coming out? He comes out to defy Israel. The king will give great wealth to the man who kills him. He will also give him his daughter in marriage and will exempt his family from taxes in Israel."
>
> David asked the men standing near him, "What will be done for the man who kills this Philistine and removes this disgrace from Israel? Who is this uncircumcised Philistine that he should defy the armies of the living God?"

They repeated to him what they had been saying and told him, "This is what will be done for the man who kills him." (1 Samuel 17:25–27)

Unlike the other Israelites, who cowered in fear at the sight of Goliath, David filled with righteous indignation. He wanted to know what would be done for the man who killed Goliath, because he saw him and what he represented as a disgrace against Israel. But just as David was learning what the reward was, his oldest brother, Eliab, saw him.

When Eliab, David's oldest brother, heard him speaking with the men, he burned with anger at him and asked, "Why have you come down here? And with whom did you leave those few sheep in the wilderness? I know how conceited you are and how wicked your heart is; you came down only to watch the battle."

"Now what have I done?" said David. "Can't I even speak?" (1 Samuel 17:28–29)

When Eliab looked at David, he saw him as insignificant. To him, he was just shepherding a few sheep. Not only that, he castigated David's character as conceited and wicked. Whereas others probably would have allowed embarrassment to make them withdraw from the situation and run home, David's history of being overlooked, not invited, discarded, and disregarded had prepared him for this moment. Instead of crumbling beneath the weight of his brother's rejecting words, David simply anchored his identity in God and kept doing what Eliab disapproved of.

In response to Eliab's rejection, "[David] then turned away to someone else and brought up the same matter, and the men answered him as before. What David said was overheard and reported to Saul, and Saul sent for him" (1 Samuel 17:30–31).

Slow down and read what just happened. The Bible says that after Eliab's withering, degrading, and discarding words to David, David simply turned away and kept asking about Goliath. Because David kept asking those questions, someone overheard what he was saying and reported it to Saul. And because that person reported it to Saul, Saul ended up authorizing David to fight Goliath. When you OPEN the gift of rejection, you will learn a valuable lesson. *People can reject you no matter what you do, so do what God says!*

People can reject you no matter what you do, so do what God says!

Eliab asked David, "Who do you think you are?" He questioned David's character and even degraded the worthiness of his vocation as a shepherd. But it wasn't Eliab's approval that made David worthy to fight Goliath; it was God's. Place your identity in who God says you are and what God says you can do.

Stop feeling bad about yourself because he left you. Keep moving forward.

Stop feeling bad about yourself because they overlooked you. Keep moving forward.

Stop feeling bad about yourself because they didn't invite you. Keep moving forward.

Don't let rejection change you, let it *anchor* you.

OPEN THE GIFT

Take a moment to identify a past or present rejection experience to which you can apply the OPEN framework to help you discover how it anchors your identity.

Observe

Take a moment to observe your thoughts about the role your rejection experience has played in anchoring your identity:

1. What lie have you believed that made you try to be someone you're not? Considering what you read in this chapter, what *truth can you use to combat* the lie you've been believing?
2. What one mental talk track have you been rehearsing that has made you believe that changing yourself would have prevented rejection from happening?
3. In what ways did you change to try to make a situation work?
4. After considering how God uses rejection to anchor your identity, what parts of your identity do you need to reclaim to get back to who God created you to be?

Pray

We were created to be in community with others. The only thing God said was *not* good in early creation was man being alone (Genesis 2:18). The beauty of community happens when we find ourselves with people who fully accept us, making us feel seen, known, and loved. But when a community takes the form of a clique, it becomes ugly. A clique accepts you only under certain conditions, which can leave you feeling invisible and misunderstood when you don't measure up.

Every day, God invites us into a relationship with him where we are fully accepted. In fact, 1 John 3:1 says, "See what great love the Father has lavished on us, that we should be called children of God! And that is what we are! The reason the world does not know us is that it did not know him."

Take a moment to go before God with what you have observed, and pray for him to help you clearly see how he has been using rejection to anchor your identity. As a guide for your prayer time, you can offer the following prayer:

> *Lord, lift the cloud of confusion that has been shrouding my ability to clearly see myself the way you see me. I have allowed people's opinions and approval to become the mold I pour myself into instead of leaning into your truth. Help me to regain the ground I have ceded to others and return it to you. I know I can trust you with my heart and my identity.*

You are not an "extra" on the set of someone else's life. You are a child of the Most High God. You were created on purpose, with purpose. And there is no opinion about you on earth that supersedes the high value God has placed on you.

Explore
Dig a bit deeper to explore how your rejection experience has given you the gift of anchoring your identity:

1. What characteristics have you changed about yourself because of others' rejection of you?
2. How have you changed, and how has it made you feel to act in ways that are not the real you?
3. Which people have made their acceptance contingent on you becoming someone you are not?
4. In what ways could the characteristics they don't approve of be part of God's unique purpose for you?
5. What do you need to do to begin seeing yourself the way God sees you?

Name

The insights you have gained through observing your thoughts, praying for God's wisdom, and exploring the lessons from your rejection have produced a rich treasure of lessons from which to pull. Now name your next step. What one action step can you take over the next two weeks to partner with God in making your pain purposeful?

Maybe you now realize you need a new set of friends who will embrace the full expression of who you are. Pray for God to reveal who those people might be, and reach out to them over the next two weeks to begin building those relationships.

Maybe you now realize you gave up a hobby you loved because someone you were trying to get acceptance from didn't approve of it. Pick that hobby back up this week: sign up for a class, purchase the supplies, find a local club or organization where others share your interest and attend their next meeting.

Maybe you now realize that the degree you've been pursuing is your dad's dream, not yours. Although this will be tough, set a meeting this week to discuss how you feel and why you are deciding to head in a different direction.

As you thoughtfully consider how rejection is anchoring your identity, let's OPEN the fourth and final gift: drawing you closer to God.

CHAPTER

GIFT #4

Drawing You Closer to God

"Is Jesus Lord of your life, Nona?"

I was just shy of twelve years old when Pastor Mike asked me this question after youth Bible study one Wednesday night.

"I . . . I don't know."

"Have you ever professed your faith in Jesus before?"

"I don't think so . . . no, I haven't."

"You ask a lot of questions about God, and I notice how you're often one of the only kids your age standing with your hands lifted during worship. Do you want to make Jesus Lord of your life?"

"What does that mean?"

Pastor Mike lovingly shared the gospel with me that night. He walked me through the priceless gift God gave to humankind in the form of Jesus and how Jesus died for me, being nailed to the cross, despite his unimaginable agony and pain.

"Jesus died so that you could have eternal life, Nona. Making him Lord of your life means that you will follow him wherever he tells you to go. It means denying yourself and your desires so that you can bring glory to him through your life. It means placing your faith in Jesus no matter what."

The thought of Jesus dying for me moved me so deeply that I started to cry. Before joining that church on a nondescript road near my neighborhood, I hadn't experienced what it was like to be wanted and loved. I had accepted my mother's words as truth—that I wasn't wanted, that she would have been better off if I hadn't been born. My church family gave me a safe place to belong, and I wanted the love of Jesus more than anything.

"Will you pray with me, Pastor Mike? I want to follow Jesus." That night, in a wood-paneled classroom of a small church in Jacksonville, Florida, I accepted Jesus as lord of my life.

After my friend who had introduced me to the church moved away, I would catch a ride to church with Pastor Mike and his family. When they dropped me off at home later that night, I walked through the front doors feeling like a new person. But, although I was a new person thanks to the saving grace of Jesus, I was still living in an old circumstance.

"Where have you been!" my mom yelled.

"At Bible study. I told you about it before I left earlier."

"For three hours? Doing what? With who?"

"Learning about God . . . and the Bible. Pastor Mike. He wants to meet you."

"Meet me for what? To tell me I'm a bad person for not

going to their church? Heck no. You've probably told them a bunch of lies about me anyway."

"No . . . I haven't told them anything about you. When they've asked about you coming to church, I've told them you have to work."

"Oh, great! So now you have them thinking I don't go to church because I'm greedy! You know what, you're not going back there."

My heart broke in half. I had finally found a place where I felt loved and seen, and my mom decided to take it from me for no other reason than a delusion she held.

"I don't understand. Why? They're nice people! I love going to church." I started to cry as anger swelled within me.

"I don't have to explain myself to you! You're not going to be making me look bad. You can tell them they don't need to pick you up anymore. That's it."

As she turned to walk away from me, I felt a rage churning inside me that I had never felt before. Years of physical and verbal abuse that had been stored deep within my heart boiled over into an emotional meltdown. When I reached my room and met a closed door, without even thinking I kicked it down, clean off the hinges. My mom heard the crash and came running to see what had happened.

"*What did you do to my door?*" she yelled. "Get out! Get out now!"

"I'm sorry! I don't know what happened! I'm sorry. I don't know where to go!"

"I don't care where you go! Get out!"

It was almost ten o'clock on a school night, and I couldn't think clearly as she lunged toward me and grabbed my right arm. She twisted it behind my back as she pushed me to the front door and out. She slammed the door and locked it behind her.

I walked aimlessly around our neighborhood for a while with hot tears streaming down my face. My eyes burned and my head hurt as I finally made my way to my classmate Lindsey's house and rang the doorbell. When her mom opened the door and saw the state I was in, she immediately asked me what had happened as she welcomed me inside. I told her my mom had kicked me out, and when she asked why, all I could say was the truth: "Because I went to church."

She prepared a plate of food from the leftovers of their dinner. Since everyone was already in bed, she brought out a pillow and blanket for me and laid it on the couch.

"I'm so sorry, Nona. I . . . I don't understand this, but we're here to help however we can."

"Thank you," I said as she turned off the lights.

In the quiet darkness of the room, hopelessness swallowed me whole. How would I go to school tomorrow wearing the same clothes I wore that day? I didn't have anything to do my hair with. I didn't even have my book bag or school supplies. My eleven-year-old mind couldn't think past the next day, and it seemed impossible for it to be a good one. But in the midst of my pain, I remembered the first sermon I'd heard my pastor preach. It was based on Psalm 68:5: "A father to the fatherless, a defender of widows, is God in his holy dwelling."

I pulled the blanket tight around my body and whispered into the stillness, "God. Help me."

EMPTY CORNERS

The apostle Paul is known as one of the greatest church plant-ers of all time because his evangelistic efforts catalyzed the wildfire-like growth of the early church. Some scholars say he directly launched fourteen churches, but when you take into account the churches that came out of those churches, you quickly realize that almost every church on earth can be traced back to his work. How strange, then, that after touching countless lives, Paul would end up near death in a Roman prison with no one in his corner.

As he sat in the squalor of his jail cell, he penned a few letters to his protégé Timothy, a young man he had adopted as a spiritual son. The letters contained theological wisdom and practical knowledge, with the goal of helping Timothy grow as a minister. The words found in 2 Timothy 4 are particularly heartbreaking. Paul tells Timothy, "Do your best to come to me quickly, for Demas, because he loved this world, has deserted me and has gone to Thessalonica. Crescens has gone to Galatia, and Titus to Dalmatia. Only Luke is with me. Get Mark and bring him with you, because he is helpful to me in my ministry" (2 Timothy 4:9–11).

Paul urgently needed Timothy's presence. His co-laborers had all deserted him in his time of greatest need. He had no one to help him, so he wrote to the only person he knew he could count on, Timothy: "Alexander the metalworker did me a great deal of harm. The Lord will repay him for what he has done. You too should be on your guard against him, because he strongly opposed our message" (2 Timothy 4:14–15).

Although Paul doesn't share particulars, some Bible scholars believe that whatever Alexander did may have led to Paul's imprisonment. Given Paul's warning to Timothy to stay on guard against him, I believe it too. Alexander's strong opposition to Paul's ministry could have been the factor that led Roman guards to arrest him. Paul tells Timothy that Alexander hurt him so deeply that only God could repay him for the harm he caused. He goes on to say, "At my first defense, no one came to my support, but everyone deserted me . . ." (2 Timothy 4:16).

When Paul looked to his corner of the ring for the fight he was in, he found it empty. No one was there when the charges were read. No one was there to provide a character witness. Paul was entirely alone. Or was he?

> ". . . may it not be held against them. But the Lord stood at my side and gave me strength, so that through me the message might be fully proclaimed and all the Gentiles might hear it. And I was delivered from the lion's mouth. The Lord will rescue me from every evil attack and will bring me safely to his heavenly kingdom. To him be glory for ever and ever. Amen." (2 Timothy 4:16–18)

Paul found himself in a dire circumstance, facing imminent execution (2 Timothy 4:6–8).

He was rejected and abandoned by the people he had broken bread with.

He was left to die by people he had spread the good news of Jesus with.

He was weak and broken in his body from the harshness of his torture.

Yet, when Paul's corner was empty, he didn't hold a grudge against the people who had abandoned him. Instead, Paul took heart in the knowledge that though his corner was *physically* empty, it was *spiritually* full through the power of God (2 Timothy 4:16–18).

When everyone walks away, God's faithfulness remains.

When everyone walks away, God's faithfulness remains.

When your child stops speaking to you, God still speaks to you.

When your friends no longer check on you, God still sees you.

When your job application gets denied, God still approves of you.

When your significant other calls it quits, God still chooses you.

When your father says you aren't his, God still claims you as his own.

And because of God's consistent faithfulness in the face of people's rejection, you can learn to do what Paul did: place your hope in God. When those closest to Paul rejected him at the height of his church-planting work, he didn't turn inward and blame himself. Instead, he allowed the pain of rejection to be a GPS that helped him navigate to the faithfulness of God.

In the same breath that he forgave his co-laborers for abandoning him, he recognized the goodness of God. He acknowledged that it was the Lord who stood by him when everyone else disappeared. He declared the consistency of God's character in delivering him from every evil attack and creating safety. He gave God glory in the midst of his pain because he had come to know the true nature of God.

When Jesus was betrayed by Judas and abandoned by Peter, the disciple who said he would never leave him even if it cost him his life, he didn't turn inward and wonder what he did wrong. Instead, he allowed what he knew about the Father to lead his thoughts upward. When Jesus found himself overcome with sorrow in Matthew 26:39, he "fell with his face to the ground and prayed, 'My Father, if it is possible, may this cup be taken from me. Yet not as I will, but as you will.'" In the midst of his pain, Jesus placed his trust in a Father whose character was always good, even when life didn't feel good.

When we OPEN the gift of rejection and allow it to draw our attention to the goodness of God, hopelessness and loneliness have to bow to the hope and presence of our sovereign God. How striking that not only Paul came to know God as the one who delivered him from the lion's mouth (2 Timothy 4:17), but David did too, giving him the courage to fight Goliath.

When Saul doubted that David could defeat Goliath, David said to him, "The LORD who rescued me from the *paw of the lion and the paw of the bear* will rescue me from the hand of this Philistine" (1 Samuel 17:37, emphasis added). David did not draw courage from military training. He didn't draw courage from an arsenal of weapons. He didn't draw courage from the size of Israel's army. Like Paul, his strength came from knowing the faithfulness of God.

But how do you get to know the faithfulness of God?

As Job was grappling with the catastrophic loss of all his children and everything he had, he said, "My ears had heard of you but now my eyes have seen you" (Job 42:5). *Job's trial drew him closer to God.*

As the Jerusalem churches under James's jurisdiction were experiencing poverty and persecution, he wrote, "Consider it pure joy, my brothers and sisters, whenever you face trials of many kinds, because you know that the testing of your faith produces perseverance" (James 1:2–3). *James promised their trials would draw them closer to God.*

As the twelve disciples were overcome by confusion at Jesus's revelation that he would be gone soon, he turned to them and said, "I have told you these things, so that in me you may have peace. In this world you will have trouble. But take heart! I have overcome the world" (John 16:33). *Jesus assured them that their trials would draw them closer to God.*

The paradox of growing your faith is that you can't grow your faith unless you *need* to grow it. Growing your faith necessitates situations and circumstances that require you to exercise it. *Rejection is like a faith gym.*

Rejection is like a faith gym.

Just as growing physical strength requires exerting enough effort to tear muscle fibers so they can grow back stronger, growing spiritual strength requires exerting enough faith to obey God when your human inclination is to give up or get even. It requires remembering that God can work all things together for your good.

Even when it seems impossible.

Even when it seems hopeless.

Even when it seems futile.

When you thought things were going great, but then your love interest stops responding to your texts and calls, their rejection is like handing you a set of spiritual dumbbells.

When you invite all your neighbors to your home for a get-to-know-you potluck, but no one shows up, their rejection is like throwing you on a spiritual treadmill at a sprinter's pace.

When you believed that award had your name on it, but the person you considered your nemesis was chosen instead, the rejection is like tying a spiritual weight belt around your waist . . . connected to a semitruck.

When rejection landed Paul in his prison cell and when rejection landed David in a field by himself, instead of allowing their confusion and pain to separate them from God, they allowed their confusion and pain to lead them into the arms of God. And they received victory.

Instead of asking, "Why did this happen to me?" train yourself to ask, "God, how do you want me to grow from this?"

EYES ON THE PRIZE

When I woke up the next morning on Lindsey's couch, I smelled bacon cooking and heard voices speaking softly in the kitchen. I got up and walked toward them to find Lindsey's parents sipping coffee at the table.

"Good morning, Nona," her father said. "Did you sleep okay last night?"

"Yes, thank you."

"I'm making breakfast now and put some clothes on

the counter over there for you," Lindsey's mom said as she pointed to a small pile of clothes. "I had to guess your size, so I apologize if they don't fit right."

"Thank you," I said.

"I also put a toothbrush and toothpaste on the bathroom counter with a washcloth and soap so you can get cleaned up."

Lindsey walked into the kitchen and looked puzzled as she saw me standing there. "Um . . . hey, Nona. What are you doing here?"

"We're taking her to school with us this morning," her mom answered quickly.

"Oh . . . okay. Are you eating breakfast with us too?"

"Yes. I just need to run to the bathroom and get changed. I'll be back in a minute."

As I walked to the bathroom, I overheard her mom trying to explain the craziness of the night before to Lindsey. When I came back out, Lindsey smiled and said, "I'm so glad you're here."

After breakfast, we loaded up our things to head out. As we drove near my house, I noticed my mom's car was gone, so I asked to stop the car. I rang the doorbell and when Lee came to the door, I asked him if I could get my backpack. Once back in the car, I felt my body start to relax. My anxiety decreased the closer we got to school.

I spent three days with Lindsey's family, and they never pressured me to go home. Since they didn't know my mom and because the circumstances of my arrival were concerning, they simply integrated me into their family rhythms and made me feel loved. As I look back on that time, I can see the hand of God so clearly. I had thought I was wandering aimlessly around my neighborhood until I "happened" upon my classmate's house, but I now understand that the Spirit guided me to the very place I needed to be to experience peace that night.

After getting dropped off at school by Lindsey's mom on the third day, I was told by one of the administrators to go to the front office. When I arrived, my mom was standing there. "*Where have you been?*" she whisper-yelled at me.

"You told me to get out."

"I didn't tell you to get out! You left and didn't tell me where you were going!"

"Huh? You told me to get out in the middle of the night!"

"I would never do that! You just need to be back home after school today. You got it?"

She walked away before I could gather my thoughts enough to respond. I was stunned. Confused. Angry. Yet again, she'd blown up my world, then blamed me for it, a pattern I'd known for as long as I could remember. As I walked to class that morning, I began praying for strength to withstand the turmoil until I could move out once and for all. I asked God to help me stay focused on the big goal: going to college. I decided that I would do everything I could to get the grades needed for a full scholarship so I could move out after graduation. *Rejection can become the fuel for your purpose.*

Rejection can become the fuel for your purpose.

Pastor Mike's middle daughter went to my school, so I told her I couldn't go to church with them anymore. When she asked why, all I could say was that my mom wouldn't allow it. When Sunday rolled around, instead of getting dressed for church, I turned on the television to watch Nickelodeon. But as I scrolled through the channels, I saw a man wearing a beautiful robe, preaching in what looked like a church made of crystal. He had a kind face, so I decided to watch him. I learned at the end of the program that the show was called *Hour of Power* and the pastor's name was Dr. Robert Schuller.

Dr. Schuller became my de facto pastor in the absence of a church. I watched him faithfully week after week, and during every show I felt like his words were reaching through the screen and strengthening my heart. During one particular sermon, he reminded viewers that God's goodness is made clearest through the bad experiences we endure. I nodded along with him as he encouraged my heart to hang in there.

Although my mother continued to be physically, verbally, and emotionally abusive, I committed to spend daily time in God's Word and in prayer. Being an only child, I had no one to vent to, so I learned out of necessity how to do what Peter said: "Cast all your anxiety on him because he cares for you" (1 Peter 5:7). When my mother yelled at me or called me names, I took my tears to God in prayer. When anger would start to boil within my heart, I took my animosity to God in confession. I was learning to turn upward instead of inward, and that practice began digging a well of hope in me from which I derived the spiritual strength I needed to survive.

By the time I entered high school, I was so focused on the vision of moving away for college that I enrolled in every Advanced Placement (AP) class the school offered. AP classes carried college credit, so every class I successfully completed translated to three credit hours of college-level coursework. While my classmates were taking art or PE for electives, I took AP Physics, AP Anatomy and Physiology, AP Chemistry, AP Spanish, AP Calculus, and more. By graduation, I had enough credits to start college as a sophomore. Not only that, but the University of Florida rewarded my high GPA and strong extracurricular involvement by giving me a full academic scholarship.

On the day I was scheduled to move away, I loaded my car and my mom's car with all my things, and we hit the road. About twenty minutes into the drive, I looked in the rearview mirror and couldn't see my mom driving behind me anymore. I figured she'd been caught at a red light, so I kept driving. When I arrived on campus an hour and a half later, I started unloading my car by myself. As my smiling dorm mates and their families unloaded cars and vans around me, I made multiple trips up and down four flights of stairs by myself. After two hours of hauling my things upstairs and unpacking, I called the house.

"Hello?" my mom answered.

"Mom, why aren't you here?"

"Look, I'm not U-Haul. I'm not driving an hour and a half to move your stuff. It's your stuff, so *you* move it."

"Okay," I said.

A mixture of exhaustion and determination filled my heart. It was after 10:00 p.m., but I decided to make the drive back to Jacksonville to get my things. When I arrived near midnight, the house was dark. I walked inside and took my mom's car keys off the counter, then went out to her car and opened her trunk to get my things. After I moved everything from her car into my car, I removed the house key from my key ring and placed it with her car keys on the counter. Then I let myself out for the last time.

As I drove back to campus, a passage of Scripture I had memorized over the previous school year ran through my mind: "Brethren, I count not myself to have apprehended: but this one thing I do, forgetting those things which are behind, and reaching forth unto those things which are before, I press toward the mark for the prize of the high calling of God in Christ Jesus" (Philippians 3:13–14 KJV).

I didn't know what my future held, but I knew God so intimately that I had peace in the unknown. The same God who had protected my mind and heart during my abuse was the same God who had given me a fully paid ticket out of a past that now lay behind me. I had kept my eyes on the prize of college for years, and as the dark stretch of road lay in front of me, I smiled at the realization that the prize wasn't that I was going to college *for free*. The prize was that I was going to college *free in Jesus*.

TURNING UPWARD

When we experience rejection, many of us instinctively turn inward—blaming ourselves, ruminating on what we did wrong, and feeling like the bad guy. This is especially true when the *other* person blames us for being the cause of their rejection.

I was sitting in my office one morning when my cell phone lit up with a friend's name.

"Nona, guess what?" Tina excitedly blurted into the phone.

"What?"

"I got selected for the County Humanitarian of the Year award!"

I was a couple of years into a new leadership role at the utility company where I worked when I met Tina. We became friends after serving on a few of the same community boards together. She was well respected in our community, and after we became friends, she called whenever she had good news to share, which was often.

"Oh, wow, Tina! That's amazing! You're so deserving!"

"I'm so excited! I was apparently nominated by multiple people. The gala is in two months. I'll need to go shopping for the perfect gown."

"You're going to look amazing. I'm so proud of you!"

"Yes, it's going to be a big night. How are you?"

"I'm doing good. I had to—"

"Oh, hey," Tina abruptly said. "Let me call you back."

"Oh . . . okay . . ."

Whenever Tina called, it was the same drill on rinse and repeat. She would share news about an award or recognition she was receiving, and I would listen to her without interruption, only interjecting to congratulate her. When I would begin to share something about myself, she would inevitably interrupt with, "Let me call you back." Days or weeks would go by without a return call, until she had more exciting news she wanted to share.

The first few times it happened, I figured she just had a lot on her plate and had to go. But, when it became a pattern,

I decided to ask her not to do it anymore. One day, after she cut me off as usual, I texted her and asked her to allow time for me to share the next time she called because friendship is a two-way street.

Apparently, that ask was too much for her. My phone immediately rang. "What's your problem, Nona?" she said.

"Huh? No problem. I would like to share about my day or life too. I feel like you rush me off the phone when I start to talk."

"I talk to you more than I talk to almost anyone, so how can you say that?" she yelled into the phone. "I give you more time than I give to anyone. How can you be so ungrateful? Besides, I have a busy life! I thought you were a friend."

I couldn't believe my ears.

She continued to talk for ten minutes straight, explaining away my concern and telling me it was selfish to expect more from her than she was giving. To add insult to injury, at the time of the call, my oldest son had been hospitalized twice in thirty-six hours, leaving me especially emotionally vulnerable. Instead of being a good friend and making sure I was okay, Tina used that situation to tell me the real problem was that I was emotionally unstable.

No matter what I said, Tina turned the situation back on me and said I was the problem. She even went so far as to use Scripture to say I needed to be humble. After I continued to try to explain over the phone, and later with text, what I was feeling, she dug in her heels even further and blamed me for being the problem. When she suddenly stopped responding to my texts, I felt confused, crushed, and rejected. Do you know what that's like?

You try to tell your boyfriend that it bothers you when he likes other women's provocative posts on social media. Instead of hearing you out and committing to change, he blames you for being insecure and says the real problem is that you have "daddy issues."

You try to tell your coworker about being harassed by your supervisor, because you need a boost of courage to file a formal complaint. Instead of encouraging you, he tells you why your clothing is tempting to a man and that you shouldn't be surprised to face harassment given what you wear.

You try to tell your teenage child that you're taking their cell phone because you're disappointed in their choices after finding explicit and inappropriate text messages. Instead of taking responsibility for their actions, they say they hate you for always sticking your nose in their business and slam their bedroom door. Even though part of the agreement for you to buy the phone was that they promised to use it with integrity, they think the problem is that you're too nosey, not that they broke the agreement.

When we don't know differently, other people's assessment can become our reality, leading us to question ourselves. *But just because someone ships their blame in your direction doesn't mean you have to accept their package.*

There is a term in psychology called *gaslighting* that, according to Psychology Today, "is an insidious form of manipulation and psychological control. Victims of gaslighting are deliberately and systematically fed false information that leads them to question what they know to be true, often about themselves."[1] Gaslighting is designed to make you question your reality by blaming *you* for problems you identify. By calling your judgment into question, a gaslighter can make you believe that the only problem is the way you see things.

Training yourself to turn your mind and heart upward in the face of rejection is a critical part of avoiding this type of manipulation.

In Garth Stein's book *The Art of Racing in the Rain*, he says, "In racing, they say that your car goes where your eyes go. The driver who cannot tear his eyes away from the wall as he spins out of control will meet that wall; the driver who looks down the track as he feels his tires break free will regain control of his vehicle."[2] If you allow others to fix your eyes on your perceived flaws, your attention and energy will be fixed on your flaws. You will believe you are a failure because you are focusing on perceived failures. But if you fix your eyes on the goodness of God, your attention and energy will be fixed on his goodness.

What you fix your eyes on determines where you go.

> **What you fix your eyes on determines where you go.**

When Saul tried to focus David's eyes on his inability to match Goliath's physical strength, David fixed his eyes on the fact that "the LORD who rescued me from the paw of the lion and the paw of the bear will rescue me from the hand of this Philistine" (1 Samuel 17:37).

Instead of fixing his eyes on the people who deserted him, Paul fixed his eyes on the truth that "the Lord will rescue me from every evil attack and will bring me safely to his heavenly kingdom. To him be glory for ever and ever. Amen" (2 Timothy 4:18).

Focusing our attention on God draws us nearer to him.

When we fix our eyes on the goodness of God in the midst of our rejection, our hearts and minds can't help but follow us there. *Focusing our attention on God draws us nearer to him.*

FULL-CIRCLE GOD

On a Tuesday morning in the spring of 2021, I received an email that made me stop in my tracks.

I had just returned from speaking in Australia and was getting my day started with a series of back-to-back video conferences. I glanced quickly at my inbox to scan for any fires that needed my immediate attention when I saw this email subject: "Hour of Power Invitation."

I hadn't heard the phrase *Hour of Power* since watching the show faithfully as a child when my mom forbade me from going to church. When I opened the email and read it, my heart filled with emotions: "Hi, Mrs. Jones. My name is Brenda, and I'm a producer for *Hour of Power*. I'm writing on behalf of Pastor Bobby Schuller to invite you to be our guest speaker in August. If you're interested, please let me know. We have been following your ministry and would love to have you."

I read the email at least ten times and even checked the email address to make sure it was authentic. I couldn't believe God had placed me on the heart of the *Hour of Power* team.

I didn't know Pastor Schuller or anyone on their team, but God made a way for me. I quickly accepted with deep humility and gratitude.

As we got closer to the date I was scheduled to speak at the church, I found myself in 1 Samuel 13–14. It was an interesting time in Israel's history. They had no iron weapons because the Philistines had ensured there were no blacksmiths available to make them (1 Samuel 13:19–21). The only people who had a sword or spear were King Saul and his son Jonathan. As I read the story, I was struck by how, despite having the same tools, Saul and Jonathan used them in completely different ways.

The Bible says in 1 Samuel 14:2 that "Saul was staying on the outskirts of Gibeah under a pomegranate tree in Migron. With him were about six hundred men." His sword and his spear were safely tucked away as he relaxed under a pomegranate tree.

Jonathan, on the other hand, had different plans. In 1 Samuel 14:6 it says, "Jonathan said to his young armorbearer, 'Come, let's go over to the outpost of those uncircumcised men. Perhaps the LORD will act in our behalf. Nothing can hinder the LORD from saving, whether by many or by few.'" In other words, Jonathan decided to head to the fight because he knew he didn't need weapons or armies if he had God's protection.

I found the juxtaposition of these two men striking because, to me, it showed the difference between knowing *of* God and *knowing* God.

When you know *of* God, you place your faith in *your* limited resources.

When you *know* God, you place your faith in *his* limitless resources.

When the day arrived to preach on *Hour of Power*, I stood on the platform that had been a source of healing for me many years ago. I was overwhelmed with gratitude and briefly shared why it was so personally meaningful to be there. And as I preached my sermon, "Give Them Your Weapons," I had a full-circle moment. I was not only preaching to the audience and viewers, I was also preaching to myself, realizing that God would continue to win battles for me, as he had done since I was a child.

Even when you have to go it alone like Jonathan did, you can place your faith in the God who protects you. Your faith in him will move you in the direction of his will for your life. Even when people try to undermine you like the Philistines did to Israel, you can place your faith in the God who doesn't need weapons or armies to win battles. Why? Because nothing can hinder God from saving, whether by many or by few (1 Samuel 14:6). Because when God is for you, no one can be against you (Romans 8:31). Because Jonathan placed his faith in God's faithfulness, God sent victory through Jonathan that day (1 Samuel 14:23).

God is forever faithful.

OPEN THE GIFT

Take a moment to identify a past or present rejection experience. Apply the OPEN framework to it to help you discover how it can draw you nearer to God.

Observe

Take a moment to observe your thoughts about the role your rejection experience has played in drawing you nearer to God:

1. What lie have you believed about this rejection that has separated you from God? Considering what you read in this chapter, what *truth can you use to combat* the lie you've been believing?
2. What one mental talk track have you been rehearsing about your rejection that is making it difficult for you to see the goodness of God through your pain?
3. What story have you told yourself to explain why a sovereign God would let your rejection happen?
4. After considering how God uses rejection to draw you closer to him, in what ways has this story led you to seek God more (or less)?
5. How has your rejection shaped your belief about God's love for you?

Pray

I have found it to be true that the pain of rejection can affect our closeness to God. For some of us, because of our anger or bitterness, rejection becomes a wedge that separates us from God. For others of us, rejection becomes a slide that accelerates our fall into his arms. I believe that how it affects us depends on what we believe about God's character.

Paul penned many of his encouraging epistles from prison, including Romans 8:38–39, where he says, "For I am convinced that neither death nor life, neither angels nor demons,

199

neither the present nor the future, nor any powers, neither height nor depth, nor anything else in all creation, will be able to separate us from the love of God that is in Christ Jesus our Lord."

When you find yourself in a hopeless situation, you can tap into hope only if you carry the wellspring of hope within you. Paul certainly did.

Take a moment to go before God with what you have observed, and pray for him to help you clearly see how he has been using rejection to draw you closer to him. As a guide for your prayer time, you can offer the following prayer:

Lord, draw me close to you as I explore the lessons you want to teach me from my pain. Remind me that you are good, even when my situation is not. Remind me that you are kind, even when the people around me are not. Remind me that you are faithful, even when my faith in people is broken. Help me to keep my eyes fixed on who you are and where you are working in my life so that my heart and mind can meet you there.

God is as near as your next breath. Inhale his peace and exhale your pain. He is waiting with open arms to receive you.

Explore

Dig a bit deeper to explore how your rejection experience has given you the gift of drawing you closer to God:

1. How has this experience caused you to seek understanding from God?

2. How often were you praying before this experience, and how has this experience caused you to pray differently?
3. What reasons for gratitude has this situation uncovered for you, and in what ways have you expressed appreciation to God?
4. What Scripture passages have you meditated on to help train your thoughts to stay fixed on the goodness of God?
5. In what new ways have you been practicing your faith to keep your heart uplifted in spite of your pain?

Name

The insights you have gained through observing your thoughts, praying for God's wisdom, and exploring the lessons from your rejection have produced a rich treasure of lessons from which to pull. Now name your next step. What one action step can you take over the next two weeks to partner with God in making your pain purposeful?

Maybe you now realize you have been more consumed with who hurt you than meditating on God's goodness in the situation. Take five minutes every morning over the next two weeks to think about and write one new reason you are grateful to God (Philippians 4:6–8).

Maybe you now realize you have spent more time telling people about your *pain* than confessing God's *promises*. Commit to studying the promises God makes to his children in Scripture, and confess three promises per day out loud (Isaiah 61:3; Psalm 23; Romans 8:28).

Maybe you now realize you have been struggling by

yourself to manage your pain. Make plans to join a coworker, neighbor, or family member for church this Sunday.

You are never alone when the loving God is your companion. Look up!

CONCLUSION

The Gift Worth Giving

I am about to break a cardinal rule of writing for this conclusion. I am going to *write about writing* (clutch the pearls).

Smack in the middle of finalizing chapter 10, I joined a virtual book club of women in Ohio who had been reading my book *Killing Comparison* together. The discussion was a nice mental break for me because, by the time it started at 7:30 p.m., I had been writing for nine and a half hours straight. Bring on the smiling faces!

I always enjoy spending time with the people who read my books because it gives me a chance to hear what they are thinking and feeling as they process my writing. The group asked wonderful questions and shared uplifting stories about how *Killing Comparison* helped them wrestle through feelings of inadequacy. Just before the call ended, a beautiful woman named Terry asked, "So, what's your writing process? How do you find time to write given your many responsibilities?"

After thinking about it for a moment, I said, "To be

honest, I don't know that I really have a *process*. I just pray . . . and write."

Transparent moment. As I allowed this book to release itself through my fingers, there were several places where I had to resist the urge to hit delete as I wrote about my experiences with my mom, my experience with Michael, and even a couple of experiences in my career. Dredging up many of those memories triggered feelings of shame. But the reason why I ultimately decided to leave them in this book is because shame gains power when we deny our story.

Which brings me to you. What parts of your own rejection story are you tempted to keep hidden out of shame or embarrassment?

What parts of your story are you praying that the passage of time will allow you to forget?

What parts of your story are you hoping to process privately so you can maintain an image of strength in the face of your pain?

While there are gifts in your rejection for *you*, there are *also* gifts in your rejection for *others*. As my written story comes to a close, I want to challenge you to begin sharing your own story because your story has power. Revelation 12:10–11 says,

> For the accuser of our brothers and sisters,
>   who accuses them before our God day and night,
>   has been hurled down.
> They triumphed over him
>   by the blood of the Lamb
>   and by the word of their testimony.

What does this mean? It means that when the shame and embarrassment of your rejection rears its head, you can triumph over its lies through the truth found in Christ *and* by sharing your testimony of victory.

When the lie of rejection says, "You're not wanted," the truth in Christ says you are accepted (John 15:15; 1 Corinthians 12:27; Ephesians 1:5). You can testify about the people who walked away from you because your value is found in the One who never leaves you or forsakes you.

When the lie of rejection says, "You're not good enough," the truth in Christ says you have been chosen by God (Matthew 5:13–14; John 15:16; 1 Corinthians 3:16). You can testify about the people who overlooked you because your significance is based on the One who died for you while you were still a sinner.

When the lie of rejection says, "You're defective," the truth in Christ says you have been made whole by God (Romans 8:1–2; Philippians 1:6; 2 Timothy 1:7). You can testify about the people who didn't choose you because you were chosen by the One who knew you before you were formed in the womb.

When you understand that no one can invalidate God's purpose for you, you become free to forgive the people who hurt you because they were never in control of your destiny anyway. You can *choose* to forgive; not because the other person is sorry and not even because they deserve it. They may not be sorry, and they may not deserve it. You choose to forgive, however, because forgiveness is its own gift. Forgiveness releases your future from the pain of your past.

You can't heal what hurts you by holding on to the hurt someone caused you. *Hurt people hurt people. Healed people heal people.*

Hurt people hurt people. Healed people heal people. As you OPEN each of the gifts your rejection has for you, my hope is that you will give the lessons you learn to others to help them find freedom from their own pain. And, along the way, my ultimate hope is that you will forgive those who hurt you in the same way you hope to be forgiven by God and others.

Every lesson you've learned in this book is for *giving* because freedom from rejection requires *forgiving*. And in that truth you will find the gift in every rejection.

ACKNOWLEDGMENTS

Before I thank anyone else, I want to thank *you*. Thank you for picking up this book and doing what I know was difficult work. Rejection is not only painful, it can also be complex. As we confront our rejection experiences, we can find ourselves peeling back an onion of rejection that has its roots in a past we thought we got over. Thank you for your courage, your vulnerability, your willingness. I pray that you have emerged from reading this book with a road map to healing. If you have, I want to hear from you. Email me at Nona@nonajones.com or message me on any of my social platforms.

This book would not even be in your hands or ears had it not been for the team at Zondervan believing I had a message worth sharing with the masses. My gratitude to Webster Younce for supporting me and quickly green-lighting this passion project of mine. To Keren Baltzer, Andrea Palpant, and Kim Tanner, thank you each for your expert editor's pen. You sharpened my ideas beautifully and chiseled away at my manuscript until what was left was exactly right.

To Katie Painter, Amanda Woods, and Matt Bray, thank you for bringing your enthusiasm, energy, ideas, and expertise to promoting this message. It was so fun to dream big together!

Yet again, my deepest gratitude is offered to my partner-in-purpose who has been my sounding board for three of my four books at this point. Thank you to my amazing friend and writing coach Margot Starbuck. You truly carry the heart of the reader, and because of this, you pushed me to go deeper so that every reader could see themselves in this work.

Similarly, I am so, so, *so* grateful to my one-hundred-plus-member #BookSquad who volunteered to read every chapter and give honest feedback so this book could be exactly what readers need. The questions you asked and critiques you offered were priceless. I also found myself inspired and encouraged by the many times you told me you saw yourself in my writing.

To Tom Dean, thank you not only for being a friend but also for being the first person to see my potential as an author those many years ago when I had about one thousand followers on Instagram. Your thought partnership and advocacy has been a gift to me.

To my family, thank you for the many hours you allowed me to steal away by myself in my office or at a beachfront hotel so I could have the mental space to write. Your support means everything to me, and I am grateful for you!

To all my friends and supporters, thank you for purchasing this book, many of you before it was even released. To the more than one million people who viewed "The Gift of Rejection" message on YouTube and reported freedom from your pain after watching it, you have been the wind beneath my wings. I read every comment—thousands of them! They encouraged me and let me know God was breathing on this message.

Last and most important, I thank God for choosing me when I felt overlooked, discarded, unwanted, and not good enough. Without him, I would have no book to write. Thank you, God, for rewriting my story.

NOTES

Chapter 3: Dangers Unseen

1. Joe Alper, "Rethinking Neanderthals," *Smithsonian Magazine*, November 17, 2013, https://www.smithsonianmag.com/science-nature/rethinking-neanderthals-83341003/.
2. Matthew Lieberman, "Why We Are Wired to Connect," Interview by Gareth Cook, *Scientific American*, October 22, 2013, https://www.scientificamerican.com/article/why-we-are-wired-to-connect/.

Interstitial: Part 2 Introduction

1. Sun Tzu, *The Art of War* (Chicago: Capstone, 2010), chapter 3, Kindle.

Chapter 4: The Root of Rejection

1. Erica Komisar, *Being There: Why Prioritizing Motherhood in the First Three Years Matters* (New York: TarcherPerigee, 2017), 3.
2. Diane Benoit, "Infant-Parent Attachment: Definition, Types, Antecedents, Measurement and Outcome." *Paediatrics & Child Health* 9, no. 8 (October 2004): 541–45, https://doi.org/10.1093/pch/9.8.541.

3. Lindsay C. Gibson, *Adult Children of Emotionally Immature Parents: How to Heal from Distant, Rejecting, or Self-Involved Parents* (Oakland, CA: New Harbinger, 2015), chapter 1, Kindle.

Chapter 9: Gift #3: Anchoring Your Identity

1. "Narcissism," *Psychology Today*, accessed March 6, 2024, https://www.psychologytoday.com/us/basics/narcissism.

Chapter 10: Gift #4: Drawing You Closer to God

1. "Gaslighting," *Psychology Today*, accessed March 5, 2024, https://www.psychologytoday.com/us/basics/gaslighting.
2. Garth Stein, *The Art of Racing in the Rain: A Novel* (New York: HarperCollins Publishers, 2009), 83.

Killing Comparison

Reject the Lie You Aren't Good Enough and Live Confident in Who God Made You to Be

Nona Jones

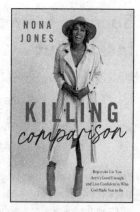

It's time to leave behind the discontent of comparative thinking and discover a free and joyful life in the security of God's love.

If you find yourself filled with feelings of insecurity, sure that others are better off or more worthy than you are . . . then you're in good company! In today's image-driven world, nearly all of us deal with the struggles of comparison and self-worth.

Nona Jones knows this mindset all too well. Throughout her life and in her recent career as an executive for the world's largest social media company, Nona discovered how true confidence can only be achieved by defeating comparative thinking and securing our identity to God's approval alone.

Join Pastor Nona Jones as she provides a fresh, biblically rooted perspective on the age-old human habit of comparing oneself to others. *Killing Comparison* will give you the tools you need to:

- Determine your true source of self-worth.
- Develop practical ways to conquer daily comparison.
- Learn how to control social media instead of letting it control you.
- Discover how to accomplish your dreams without comparing yourself at every turn.

Through practical insight and down-to-earth encouragement, Nona helps you avoid the despair of comparison and pursue a life inspired by the one who made us in his image.

Available in stores and online!

Success from the Inside Out

Power to Rise from the Past to a Fulfilling Future

Nona Jones

Join corporate executive and leadership speaker Nona Jones as she takes you on a personal journey of healing from the past so you can move forward with freedom and hope.

Many of us aspire to achieve status, wealth, and notability in the hopes that those things will erase the pain of our past. But for those who have experienced trauma, like Nona Jones, success requires more than a changed mindset—it requires repairing a broken spirit.

Nona was appointed to an executive role with a Fortune 100 company at only twenty-three years old. Since then, she has led award-winning initiatives in public affairs, brokered multimillion-dollar business deals, addressed the United Nations, and championed juvenile justice and education policy reform in the halls of Congress—all before she turned thirty-five.

Then, in one of the biggest wake-up calls of her life, Nona realized that her past battles were waging a present war. *Success from the Inside Out* charts the course of Nona's breakthrough—a course that can also lead you out of the storms of your past or present. Through her own remarkable story and insights, Nona helps you:

- Claim victory at the place where the defeat happened
- Recognize ways you use work to cover up inward brokenness
- Still the voices in your head that say you aren't good enough
- Choose fulfilling success instead of empty success
- Map your mile-markers toward your biggest goals
- Push through brokenness into a breakthrough

Available in stores and online!

From Social Media to Social Ministry

A Guide to Digital Discipleship

Nona Jones

Nona Jones, a globally acclaimed thought leader on leveraging technology for ministry, had been leading a movement and sounding the alarm for several years to make digital discipleship a central part of every church's ministry approach. In *From Social Media to Social Ministry*, she outlines her digital discipleship principles and provides practical instruction for how to do it no matter how big or small a local church may be. There are plenty of books to help churches build a social media strategy, but this is the first book of its kind that goes beyond digital marketing to digital ministry.

Readers will leave this book with:

- Clarity on what discipleship truly is
- The data that underscores the urgency for digital discipleship
- Understanding of the resources required to do it well
- A step-by-step guide on how to implement digital discipleship into ministry plans
- Knowledge of the differences among and purposes of the most popular social platforms, as well as the tools best positioned for digital ministry

Available in stores and online!

From the Publisher

GREAT BOOKS

ARE EVEN BETTER WHEN THEY'RE SHARED!

Help other readers find this one:

- Post a review at your favorite online bookseller

- Post a picture on a social media account and share why you enjoyed it

- Send a note to a friend who would also love it—or better yet, give them a copy

Thanks for reading!